Understanding Youth

T. Garvice and Dorothy Murphree

Convention Press / Nashville, Tennessee

To Chris and Brenda,
our two teen-age daughters, who have

      opened themselves to us,
      forgiven our misunderstanding,
      shared their perceptive insight,
      put us on the track of many just right books
         and articles,
      gone the second mile a hundred times in patience
         and acceptance during the writing of this book,
      and are waiting for equal time to write
         the book *Understanding Adults*.

Preface

"I am an iceburg and one fourth of me is shown to others . . ." These lines begin a study of youth. The study is probing. It moves the emotions. It stimulates the thought processes. It demands reactions.

Youth has always been a complex age to understand. Every generation has had its own communication gap with its elders. Never before, however, have there been so many reasons for misunderstandings between youth and adults.

This book, if it does it's job, will open windows on a new world and help adult workers comprehend some of the processes of growth and adjustment that all youth go through. Many of the growth pains and joys which it discusses are of the same type that adolescents have always gone through. Frequently, the adult reader will recall his own experiences and marvel at the similarities revealed in the text. At other times, he will have difficulty empathizing with today's youth.

The reader will find some themes and subjects treated which have not been treated before in Convention Press publications —not, indeed, in many media available to the average worker with Youth. Some of the subject areas will be controversial. That material which is controversial was included with only one motive in mind: to aid workers in knowing how to reach youth for the Saviour and to nurture them in their growth toward mature Christian adulthood. Special arrangements, in fact, will probably have to be made in many church groups to study chapter 2 and Appendix A in segregated groupings.

Understanding Youth is a companion book to *Guiding Youth* by Janet Burton. The two books, used together, should become rich resources to which the worker with Youth will frequently turn in his search for ways to meet the needs of his groups of young people.

—WILLIAM H. STEPHENS
Editor

Understanding Youth

Contents

Introduction xi

Part I. The Emerging Individual 1
   Chapter 1—LOOKING FOR A ME 3
   Chapter 2—GROWING UP AND OUT 21
   Chapter 3—FEELING GROOVY 29
   Chapter 4—HE'S GOT A MIND OF HIS OWN 37

Part II. Youth Learning to Relate 51
   Chapter 5—EVERYBODY'S GOTTA HAVE A HOME 53
   Chapter 6—WHERE DO I BELONG? 65
   Chapter 7—THE YOUTH CURTAIN 75
   Chapter 8—CHEMISTRY, CHAUCER, AND CHEERLEADERS 93
   Chapter 9—WHERE HAVE ALL THE OTHERS GONE? ...106

Part III. Youth's Values and Involvement 115
   Chapter 10—WHERE THE ACTION IS 117
   Chapter 11—IN THE BEGINNING GOD 125
   Chapter 12—IS THIS ALL? 143

Conclusion 153
Appendix A: Youth and Sexuality......................156
Appendix B: An Evaluation of Survey of Southern
                Baptist Youth 184
Personal Learning Activities 203
The New Church Study Course 206
   REQUIREMENTS FOR CREDIT FOR CLASS OR HOME STUDY ..207
Bibliography 210

Introduction

A WORD FROM THE AUTHORS

> I am an iceberg and only one-fourth of me
> is shown to others.
> Only one-fourth of me is above the surface of the
> inpenetrable waters that conceal my inner self . . .
> the real me.
> Does anyone dare . . .
> To search beneath those waters . . .
> Does anyone dare . . .
> To understand me?

DOES ANYONE DARE to understand the 14-year-old girl who wrote these pleading lines? Will anyone try to see her as she is: a person struggling to find out *who* she is and *why* she exists?

This book is written primarily for use by leaders and parents of Youth in the age range of twelve through seventeen. The book, admittedly, is biased in favor of these emerging young men and young women, because the authors were trying desperately to see life through *their* eyes. It is hoped, too, that sympathy for those adult men and women who give themselves to the task of leading Youth is also apparent.

We hold no claim to infallible answers to the many complex problems involved in understanding Youth.

This book will have served its purpose well if it becomes one of many resources to prod, assist, and guide you in your task of leading young people. It cannot *make* you understand or even like Youth, but perhaps the principles and ideas included in it will ignite you and propel you on an endless, exciting journey.

Do you know your Youth? Or do you simply hold on to an image of what you *hope* they are or what you *want* them to become? Some workers have the notion that "if they were like us they would be good; otherwise, they are bad." However, each Youth should be permitted to forge ahead toward adulthood in his own hope, without adult-determined identities forced upon him.

Adults have for too long regarded Youth with envy, fear, and anger because he says and does things that challenge us, or that (perhaps) we wish we had done. In a real sense, it is the adult who is rebelling against the teen-ager. "In the postwar 1940's we reacted to the noisy chest-beating of the adolescent with our usual tirade of envy, fear and anger. So the teen-ager was forced to go underground, producing the silent, surly beat generation of the 1950's . . . Now youth has reemerged loudly and clearly—clearly, that is, if we adults will look and listen, really listen, to what youth is saying about himself, us, the world." [1]

Are we willing to listen? Are we willing to try to understand Youth? To really get to know him? Most adults know Youth, if at all, only by what they do, where they go, how they dress, and by their apparent attitudes and values.

The task of the worker with Youth is to help the adolescent discover his true self as an important person created in the image of a loving God, each one being uniquely different. So, if you want to get to know and understand an adolescent, . . .

Listen to his music (they do not all like the same kind) ;
See his movies (if you are a "mature audience") ;
Frequent his eating places (if your stomach is strong) ;
Attend his ball games (you may need earplugs) ;

Chaperone his parties (when asked);
Take a trip with him (such as sponsor a choir trip,
    if you can live without sleep);
Listen when he is not speaking;
Read the writing on the walls (that is if you can read
    between the lines);
Read what they write—not just what someone else
    writes about them.

The authors delved into the findings of learned doctors, psychologists specializing in adolescence, and youth specialists, but much of their knowledge came via the above route. The writers' oldest daughter, when asked what she thought about her parents writing a book on Youth, answered, "I think it is a good idea *if* you will let a teen-ager write at least one chapter."

While we did not set aside one specific chapter for an adolescent to write, throughout the book our policy was to look and listen to what many different Youth think about themselves.

Who Is the Adolescent?

The adolescent is not a static figure. He is in motion. He is dynamic. He is changing. He doesn't stand still for measurement, study, or comparisons. He may be viewed, in some limited sense of the word, as an individual, or as a member of a group, or as a large segment of society. Regardless of *how* he is observed, he is changing even while, and in some measure as a result of, being observed.

Now is all important to youth! His greatly enlarged concept of time and space finds primary value as it relates to the *me, here,* and *now.* This characteristic is particularly true relative to materials and values. Whatever he wants, he wants *now.* Whatever he likes, he likes *now.* Whatever he considers to have value, it is of value to him personally, and is of value *now.* Even that which offers pleasure and satisfaction is not valued highly unless it offers that pleasure and satisfaction *now.* Style of dress is valuable only if it contributes to his sense of being "in" now.

Music must be now, and it must be personal. One teen-ager

yelled to his sister, "Take that record off, stupid. It was popular last month!"

Youth lives in a "no-man's land" of his own making. Mancil Ezell says, "Today's now generation feels itself suspended between the 'no more' and the 'not yet': no more child and not yet adult. Certain 'badges' of adulthood are adopted, and adapted, by youth groups to 'prove' among their peers that they are adults. Such badges are automobiles, cosmetics, personal charge accounts, personalized accessories, private club memberships, various adult-like activities." [2]

Friedenberg, in *Coming of Age,* says that the plight of the adolescent is basically similar to that of an emigrant, in that he cannot stay what he was nor ever fully become what he started out to be.

Youth may be in opposition to his parents, a threat to his leaders, in competition with his peers.

He conveniently divides people, articles, experiences into two groups; those he likes and those he doesn't. He divides adults somewhat systematically. He speaks disdainfully of customs, manners, and conditions which he dislikes, and usually fixes the blame on someone for his dislike. His value scales usually consist of extremes—tastes, habits, dress, activities—all in broad but sharply defined categories, and all subject to change, even reversal, overnight.

Can We Define Adolescence?

"Adolescence cannot be defined in physical terms, or purely in cultural terms. In adolescence, the child experiences a series of events some of which are initiated by his own body, some initiated by the people who surround him, and some initiated by his own self-system." [3]

Even though each Youth is a distinct individual who to a real extent defies classification, a knowledge of the general characteristics of adolescence can help a worker to become sensitive to ways of communicating with Youth as individuals. Each description you read fits some teen-ager. No description fits every one of them. Don't expect any one Youth to embody *all* descriptions. He'd really explode!

Dr. Carl Adatto describes adolescence as "that stage of development which begins about twelve and ends somewhere between eighteen and twenty-four years of age, depending on how long the characteristics of adolescent personality remain in force." [4] He says that *puberty* refers to the physical changes which occur about this time in life, whereas *adolescence* refers to the net interaction of the personality with the environment.

The word "adolescence" is derived from the Latin verb *adolescere*, meaning to grow, to grow to maturity. In America, we usually think of adolescence as being the period from the onset of puberty to financial independence. Puberty is a period of increased sensitivity, resentment, and irritability. It is both a stage and a process of growth.

Mancil Ezell says, "Adolescence is the period of human growth and development during which most, perhaps all, aspects of mind, emotion, and body become active and functional. In this period there occurs the greatest development of individuality, personality, sexual maturity, and release from parental control." [5]

Our industrially developed society causes the period of adolescence to be lengthened because of the increase in the number of years required to prepare for a vocation and the decrease in the need for unskilled labor. As a result, our population includes a large minority of persons who are adults in many ways, but unable to maintain economic independence.

According to Dr. Gene Usdin, there are four tasks the adolescent must accomplish as he moves toward adulthood: "He must establish his heterosexual identity, choose a vocation, emancipate himself from his parents, and commit himself to responsible citizenship." [6]

If he misses very far on any of these, he is likely to be in trouble.

The scope of this book includes only the portion of adolescence which includes the junior and senior high age group. Physically, the junior high is rapidly becoming an adult and the senior high is already one. But the Youth of either age level must learn to find meaning and fulfilment in his newly acquired and yet developing capacities. He wants to use mental faculties and mental and motor skills. He is becoming aware of mental competence among numerous competitive persons and forces.

Workers must be careful not to break the individual Youth apart into separate physical, mental, emotional, social, or psychological categories. Development in any of these areas cannot be separated from the whole. Rather each is one facet of the individual personality. The personality is singular. While various facets of growth—intellectual, physical, social, and psychological—all interact on one another and are all involved dramatically in the development of the maturing person, he still is one, and must be considered in his oneness.

Youth struggles to understand himself as he is and as he is becoming. He begins an eager search for personal peace and status in society. He uses experimentation as a primary means of learning about himself and others. He spends a lot of time daydreaming. He tests his skills, as well as his social development, through group activities. In short, he behaves, as do all other human beings, out of the urge to satisfy the needs he feels.

The *whole* Youth will be viewed in the course of this book's study, first an examination of his search for identity as he emerges from childhood into adulthood, next through a look at his culture, then at his relationships with others, and finally at his involvement and values.

Understanding any human being is difficult at any age. As workers with Youth, we will sympathize with the fourteen-year-old girl who wrote "I Am an Iceburg." We can try . . . we must try.

> I realize I can never know a person
> as you know him, God . . .
> or even as the individual knows himself.
> But I can try . . .
> And I will.

We will never understand God.
We will never understand this world.
We will never even understand one of the
many persons in this world.
But we can try . . .
We *must* try . . .
I must try.

I must explore the waters that
conceal other icebergs . . .
And help them to help themselves . . .
to find God . . .
And to understand.

1. Gene Usdin, M.D., editor, *Adolescence: Care and Counseling* (Philadelphia: J. B. Lippincott Co., 1967), p. 22.

2. A. V. Washburn, compiler, *Sunday School Work, 1968-69*, Intermediate Edition (Nashville: Convention Press, 1968), pp. 75-76.

3. Ira J. Gordon, *Human Development: From Birth Through Adolescence* (New York: Harper and Brothers, 1962), p. 268.

4. *Op. cit.*, Usdin, p. 130.

5. *Op. cit.*, Washburn, p. 72.

6. *Op. cit.*, Usdin, p. 11.

PART 1

The Emerging Individual

The human self is not a gift—
It is an achievement
                    —*Blaine M. Porter*

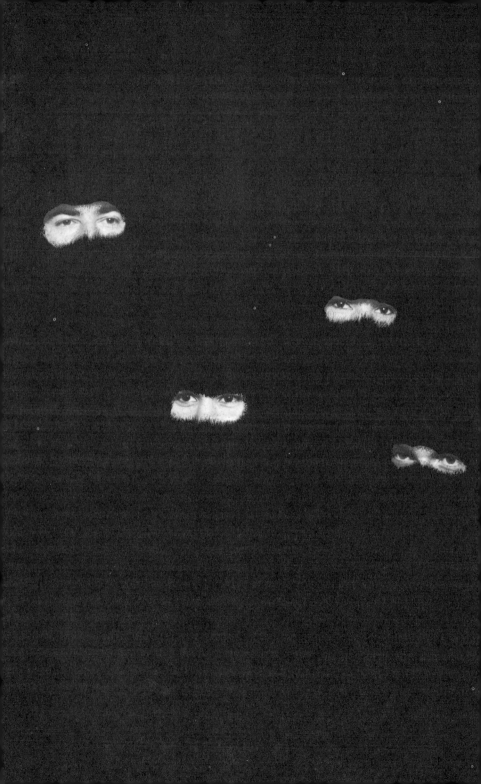

Chapter 1. LOOKING FOR A ME

DURING EARLY ADOLESCENCE, the individual is not so much saying, "Look, I'm me," but rather, "I'm *looking* for a *me*." In his search to establish his own identity, he must learn to accept his sex role as either male or female; he must learn to break away from his childish dependence on parents; he must learn to resist pressure toward wholesale conformity with his age group; and he must learn to accept himself as the person he can become. These four "tasks" are highly significant in the youth's development as an emotionally adjusted, well-rounded person. If he does not complete any one of these tasks, the result will make itself known throughout his adult life.

This search for identity can be a frustrating experience. One young man who lived with his aunt and uncle, when asked what kind of person he thought he was, answered only: *confused, stunned, hurt.* This three-word composition reveals volumes about the frustrations this boy felt in trying to establish some kind of personal identity.

A seventeen-year-old senior boy revealed a great deal about

himself when he answered this question which had been assigned for an English composition: *What kind of person do I
think I am?*

> I'm really not sure what kind of person I am ... I figure I'm
> just a kerr. [He must surely mean "cur."] Different char-
> acteristics, very varied, make up my personality. A little
> hot-headed at times, a lot stubborn, a lot clownish, a little
> stupid when my hot head boils to a peak, and a lot under-
> standing ... I would say I'm thoughtful the most, though.
> Not mainly in the sense of kind; but in the sense of think-
> ing continually. I go often to the woods or anywhere else in
> private and think. I think of my family, God, events that
> day, something that will happen, my wishes, and the world
> in general. I love to just think of nothing but my thoughts.
> I know this may sound foolish, but I enjoy this totally.

When asked to answer the question: *What kind of person do
I think other people think I am?* he wrote:

> I know I can't say or predict what others think of me ...
> I know how they would enjoy me to act, and bend my per-
> sonality to theirs ... Yes, I do bend some of my branches
> the way they do theirs, but my main tree, my personality,
> still stays somewhat the same.

A seventeen-year-old girl answered the same questions quite
differently:

> What kind of person do I think I am? I think of myself as
> a semi-sensitive person. I'm carefree and all for fun. I like
> to live, love, and be loved in return, without any hangups
> or complications.
>   What kind of a person do I think others think I am? A
> lot of people who aren't full of their own selves like me.
> They like to have fun and accept me as the flirt I am. The
> others look like they hate me, and think of me as prissy.
> But if they'd forget their criticisms and hangups they'd be
> the person I am.

When asked what kind of person she would like to be, she
said, "I'd like to be a very rich, sophisticated, sexy, beautiful,

glamorous girl. To have the world on a shoestring like a yo-yo."

Consider, in terms of self-image, what these youth each revealed. The boy said, "Different characteristics, very varied, make up my personality." To what extent is this insight typical of youth? What did he mean by his reference to "my own little world that no one else has the pleasure to view"? Do you suppose most adolescents spend as much time just plain *thinking* as he does? Is he mature in personality development? Has he made good progress toward establishing his own identity? Why or why not?

Re-read the girl's image of herself. What insight into her personality can you gain from the description of herself as semi-sensitive? What, judging by her statement, does she think of other people in general? Has she made as much progress toward establishing her identity as the boy? Do they simply want different things out of life?

These may or may not appear to be typical young people. One fact may be sure, however: they are real, live young persons. They are thinking very deeply about themselves and about others.

Very often, the adolescent becomes introspective and begins to analyze and criticize himself. It is hard for him to believe that anything about himself is good. He may wear a facade which masks his real feelings and present a different face to the world than the one he himself actually confronts. One girl expressed her feelings about herself like this:

> On the outside, I don't act the way my inside feelings tell me to. I say a lot of things I don't mean, but someone always takes it the wrong way . . . I guess other people think I'm a big flirt and just go around being mean. They just don't know me . . . Deep inside, I think I have a kind heart for those around me. I love to help people who are in trouble or just need someone to talk to.

She went on to say that she was a rebellious person because she was always being pushed into something that she didn't have any intention of doing.

As revealed in these examples, the adolescent is concerned with his spiritual life, his struggle to find himself, his need to distinguish himself from others, and his attempt to formulate a stable enough concept of himself to afford some kind of order to his life.

He has not reached the point of accepting himself as a person whose uniqueness is desirable and worthwhile. He knows that he differs from his peers, but he still feels that it is necessary to seek their acceptance and approval.

Self-esteem, an appreciation of one's own value as a person, is very much involved in the process of discovering oneself and of changing to fit the image an adolescent chooses for himself. He is more concerned with himself than he is with other people or with the social, religious, and political forces around him. This concern is especially to be noted in the younger adolescent. It also accounts for the seemingly selfish, self-centered attitude of the adolescent. He is having to give so much attention to his inner life, to the "why" of life that he has little time for anything else. He is trying to find some purpose for living. The opening number of the contemporary musical for Youth, *Purpose,* states the question well: "This life I have which is mine to live, Oh, what is it all about?" [1]

Why is it that youth today have such a difficult time "looking for a *me*"? Is it more difficult for them than for young people in preceding generations?

Too Much Too Soon in Too Short a Time

"If we adults find ourselves overwhelmed at times by the pace, the pressure, the demands of this new world, what then of the impact on the adolescent, who has never known a tranquil world, a tranquil society?" [2]

Adolescents are growing up in an age of uncertainties. They cannot predict their futures. The world itself is threatened by nuclear annihilation. In 1969, a high school sophomore—who may not be representative, but who points up the intensity of the concern—wrote:

The majority of my worries are due to the probable effect of the world's pressure upon me and the majority of young people today. My main worry is being sent to Viet Nam which I oppose as it is now being fought, undeclared and involuntarily for the most part. Running a close second is the draft which is simply a dressed-up form of slavery. Equally worrisome to me is the feeling toward youth in America. The American Youth is going to get his rights soon and I hope that it won't be by violence, although it could very easily come to that.

Another young man, also a sophomore in high school, wrote that he worried about getting a late model car. (He was about to get his driver's license and the family car was eleven years old.) After he mentioned the car, he then said:

Viet Nam is another worry. It is not a continuous worry, but one that arises in my mind every once in a while. Nobody wants to go, but I am willing if I have to. The question of world problems arises in my mind. It is more of a wonder than a worry. I wonder if the wars can be stopped. I wonder if pollution can be controlled. I wonder if there will be enough food and water to live on.

Another reason the struggle for self-identity is greater in our culture than in any other is because adult experiences are thrust upon youth so early by way of mass communications media and because they are exposed to adult patterns and problems at an accelerated rate.[3]

Even the preschooler is exposed to the soap operas with their daily rounds of sickness and death; unemployment and tight budgets; jealousy and hatred; deceit and fraud; murder and violence; falling in and out of love many times with married as well as unmarried men or women; pregnancies and childbirth; divorce and heartbreak; dope and alcoholism; unwed mothers; war and the separation it brings; along with joys, happiness, and good times of adulthood. Long before an individual reaches adolescence, he has been conditioned by a great many adult experiences.

The adolescent is exposed to too much too soon. This exposure has the effect of forcing adult responses upon him before he has been able to discover who he is. Although each generation can expect to live longer, society demands that individuals be allotted less time for youth.

One sixteen-year-old girl said, "You know, it seems that I never really had a childhood. I can't remember feeling like a child after I was seven or eight years old."

Mothers, fathers, teachers, school and community organizations, and church leaders sometimes contribute in various ways to the "big push" which sends youth headlong and puzzled from childhood securities directly into adult experiences and emotions. One reason some young people drop out of society or get lost is to avoid facing all the frightening adult experiences before they become adults.

Youth and Self-Image

Dr. Ruth Strang (*The Adolescent Views Himself*) lists four dimensions of the self or four images the youth has of himself.

1. The kind of person he thinks he is.
2. The kind of person he fears he is.
3. The kind of person he thinks others see—the social self.
4. The kind of person he would like to be or hopes to become.

This four-image idea served as a guideline for a localized research project in which the self-image of youth was explored. Ninety-three English students in a southern border state school wrote compositions in answer to these three questions:

1. How do you see yourself as a person? Or, what kind of person do you think you are?
2. What kind of person do you think other people think you are?
3. What kind of person would you like to be? What are your goals and purposes in life?

The students were identified only by age, sex, number of brothers or sisters in the family, whether they were living with one or both parents or with someone other than their parents. There were no names on the papers and the students were told that the teacher would not read their compositions. Each individual was encouraged to be completely honest in his self-evaluation.

The authors of this book quickly admit that they are not professional researchers. Their intention in gathering these responses was to give workers with Youth some insight into the images that these high school students from a county high school have of themselves.

A worker or church may want to find out if the images these young people have of themselves is typical of the way most local area youth see themselves. Educators in an area would likely be pleased to cooperate in the gathering of similar information. Or you may be able to obtain such information through the Youth of the church. The anonymity of each individual should be carefully guarded and each youth should be given reason to feel confident that such will be the case. Create the atmosphere for openness and honest evaluation.

THE KIND OF PERSON THE ADOLESCENT THINKS HE IS

The rapid changes that take place in the adolescent's height, weight, body build, and voice make it necessary for him to change his *body* image. The individual has no control over his or her basic height or bone structure. The boy has no control over his voice change. However, negative inner self-concepts may cause him to become anxious and dissatisfied with himself and those around him. The too-fat adolescent who refuses to lose weight no matter what may be saying: *The inside of me is ugly and unlovable, so I will make sure the outside me is the same.* Or, he may have such a poor self-image that he cannot trust love from others. Since he cannot love himself, he is convinced that no one else can love him. But he wants and needs to be loved so badly that he throws up this big, overweight, unattractive body as a barrier to normal everyday give-and-take love relationships. Then, if anyone (peer or adult) climbs over this barrier

and loves him in spite of his exterior, he *hopes* he can be confident that it's for real.

A positive self-concept allows the person to be more open to
the world and to accept himself and those around him.

The family's financial standing also influences the image the
youth has of himself. Finances become a tool some youth use to
acquire acceptance with a peer group. When a youth has other
ways to gain peer acceptance, such as athletics or music, finances take on less importance, but can become of great significance to the youth who has low ego strength. However,
enough money to keep up with the pace of teen-age spending is
important to any youth. When a young person does not have
money to spend in a similar fashion to his friends, he must
establish his identity in some other manner—a very difficult
and sometimes dangerous situation.

Clothes can become a symbol of acceptance and identity with
certain peer groups and friends. Manufacturers and retailers
appeal to the teen-ager's interest in clothes. There are also a
number of other signs of acceptance such as cars, sports equipment, attendance at significant social functions or restaurants,
and heavy spending.

Lack of attention to personal appearance may be an outward
manifestation of inner self-depreciation, in the same way and
with some of the same results as the overweight youth who refuses to do anything about his problem.

The family's economic situation further affects the youth's
image in his view of the value of the family car and the type
house they live in. The boy who is beginning to think of driver-
training is keenly aware of the family car or cars. One high
school sophomore boy expressed it this way:

> My biggest worry is if our family will ever get a new car
> or one that is a late model. We have '56 and '58 models now.
> I know we don't have the money, but I am conscious of the
> way I look and dress. Now that I will be driving soon, I
> want a good-looking car to go out on dates in. I am going to
> try to get a job to work up the money to buy my own car,
> but that will take a while.

Not having a place to entertain friends without feeling embarrassed decreases a person's conception of his own importance and his feeling of social competence. A girl who is a member of a "good" clique feels pretty rotten when she does not have a house adequate to take her turn hosting the bimonthly Friday night slumber party.

Young people are also concerned about their physical and mental health. Many of them express fear of cancer or emotional disturbances. "In a culture full of psychological terms, such as *adjustment* and *security*, it is no wonder that he sees his own mental health as a problem. The fact that he places mental health high on his list may be a way of telling us that he has not yet found himself and solved the problem of individuality and group living." [4]

He is seeking selfhood, but yields to group pressure. The turmoil and constant pull may cause him to fear emotional instability and physical disability.

In the following examples, this tension is apparent:

A seventeen-year-old boy.—If I had to tell what I think of myself it would be that I am friendly and nice and I respect other people. I am not handsome, but I get by with what I look like. I have mixed feelings that I cannot express to anyone because I don't know how. I try to keep my mind and body clean and strong at all times. I think I am a religious person . . . I would like to become the kind of person in my lifetime so that when I die people will say that I was a good guy in my life. And that's all.

Another teen-age boy.—I am a person who is extreme in most things and have no control over my emotions. I am average in appearance, nothing special about me. I am friendly and want to hurt no one. I am extremely jealous and self-centered. I dislike people who do not believe what I do. I like girls and can't tick without their attention, but I am a bit shy. I am the type that does all I can do to help others. I am religious, and have strong convictions. I love to have people's attention. I am a bit lonely and have a great imagination. I act dumb but I'm really not (except in my lessons) . . . I like to have a purpose behind everything I do. I am a good judge of people, and trust very few.

A teen-age girl who lived with her grandmother.—I think of myself as being a sorta mixed-up person. I really haven't determined what I want out of life yet. I don't really know what I'm looking for in this world. I seem to always be learning things the hard way. Every day appears to bring another new problem to add to my long list of problems. Life to me is a puzzle with a few pieces missing.

Another seventeen-year-old girl.—I am a person who is afraid of other people—afraid of hurting other people and afraid of being hurt myself. I have a terrible temper and often say things I don't really mean. I show my feelings too much . . . I have a habit of putting my work off until the last moment or not even doing it . . . One of my goals in life is to find out what I really believe in. Another is to find the place where I fit in. I want to be able to help other people, but first I have to find out who and what I am.

This next self-image from a teen-age boy may appear rather unusual. His social image and goals are so revealing of what he thinks about himself that his answers to all three questions are included:

What kind of person do I think I am?—I think I'm a person who has the universe—and beyond—as my scope. Rather than being overly concerned with things as they now are, I think ahead and ask myself, "Will this be here or amount to the point of being noticed a hundred years from now?" *What kind of person do others think I am?*—Others think I'm rather "stuck-up" with my head in the clouds . . . Since my views are rather unorthodox, accepting reincarnation, clairvoyance, and ESP as merely demonstrating the beautiful synchronization of the universe and the relation between one sphere or dimension and the next, I'm viewed as "odd," and I endeavor to dress accordingly. Though my morals are conventional, many of my ideas aren't.

What kind of person would I like to be?—I would like to be less materialistic, though I am considered not enough so, and would like to further develop my communicative abilities, probably more than anything else. I would like to marry, enjoying myself 90 per cent of the time, or in study, devoting only enough time to make myself financially comfortable.

THE KIND OF PERSON THE ADOLESCENT FEARS HE IS

A youth's perception of himself is usually transitory, but the adolescent may act as though this temporary elation or depression—optimism or pessimism with reference to the self— would last forever. To the adolescent, though, *today* is forever. Tomorrow seems almost out of reach.

This fear is demonstrated in the response of a fourteen-year-old girl:

> Being shy seems to be my biggest problem, as I see this worry in whatever I do and say . . . I try to talk, but after I say anything, I weigh it to see if I said anything wrong. I play the words over and over in my mind. Because I am so shy, I worry about whether people like me or not. I know some people think I'm a snob because I don't talk to them much.

THE KIND OF PERSON AS THE ADOLESCENT THINKS OTHERS SEE HIM

The adolescent tries so hard to see himself as others see him that he becomes conspicuously self-conscious. Therefore, he may elect an odd assortment of friends and associates for odd reasons. This self-consciousness also shows up in crushes, special friends, and dates—superficial interpersonal relations. He is trying to see himself reflected in their lives.

Of course, others may not see him as he thinks they see him, but the important thing is that he *believes* others think a certain way about him. Dr. Strang says that if the teen thinks people believe he is dumb or socially unacceptable, he tends to see himself in these negative ways. Or, if his friends, parents, and other adults have made him feel secure by communicating their belief in his positive qualities, he will take more hopeful attitudes toward himself.

Dr. Robert Rosenthal, a Harvard psychologist, says that one person's prediction of another person's behavior somehow comes to be realized. This expectation can be communicated to the other person in unintended ways. "I am not what I think I am, and I am not what you think I am. I am what *I think you think I am.*" [5]

The poet Goethe used different words to express the same idea when he advised, "Treat people as if they were what they ought to be and you help them to become what they are capable of being." Of course, a balance must be found between pressing a youth into a mold and providing opportunities for expression of latent abilities or talents.

A youth's response to being observed as through a looking glass depends on the expectations of the one whom he knows is watching him. The youth is reluctant to be evasive with people who expect him to be straightforward. The fact that he knows others are counting on him helps him become as good as they think he is. Leontyne Price, the great opera star, got her first job as a maid with a family who predicted that she had the makings of a great soprano. The opposite response also can be expected. If an adolescent gets assigned the role of dumbbell, wallflower, or fatty, he feels that this role is expected of him and he therefore lives up (or down) to it, with damaging results.

One young person said, "Everyone has to play the big game, cat and mouse; and put a big wall up around ourselves. If you came out of your shell with the wrong person you can be crushed ... It's a shame that we are so often not accepted for what we are but must strive to build a facade of false social fronts in order to attain certain goals." [6]

The students tested in the author's local survey answered honestly:

> *Seventeen-year-old boy* who has seven brothers and three sisters—As I look through other people's eyes, I see a tall, skinny boy. He is much self-centered. He thinks only of himself. He also has a few good points. He likes to have fun. He is a person that I would like to have as a friend.

A senior girl.—Other people don't always see the real me. They think that I mean things differently than what I really am trying to say. Sometimes they see the bad in me when it's really the good speaking or acting. And many times they see the good in me when it's really the bad working.

Teen-age girl who lives with her father, stepmother, one stepbrother, and three stepsisters—I think other people dislike me. There are many reasons why they should. I try to talk and make conversation, but I am not like most of them. Most people like to be well known or have a lot of friends. This doesn't matter to me. Most people really misunderstand me, even my parents when I mention my goal in life. I am just different.

This girl went on to say that her main goal was to help someone. She wanted to become a nurse and then serve as a missionary. She wanted to give people happiness and let them know "how wonderful God is."

One young man admitted that he still liked to go out and get a fight going or just get drunk. He answered the question about what others thought of him:

They think that I'm a nogood body. But that don't mean much. They just don't say much mean, but sometime they begin to talk about me.

But even this boy has a goal in life. He said his goal was "to get settled down and have a nice family and be a good father to my children."

THE KIND OF PERSON THE ADOLESCENT WANTS TO BECOME

"Each child has his magic mirror, too. It consists of his idealized image of what he might look like when he grows up . . . We are aware of what seems—to the adult—the inordinate amount of time the early adolescent spends in front of the mirror. Could it be that he needs this time to attempt a reconciliation between the hoped-for and the emergent reality?" [7]

The ideal self is a difficult image to focus, and involves more than daydreams. It means setting goals, deciding on purposes, and being willing to make the dreams and goals develop into realities. There are no easy streets to development of a good self-image. Some youth set this ideal self so low that it may destroy their creativity or self-esteem. Others may set their goals so high that they experience frustration and depression when they cannot reach them.

Some teens simply refuse to clarify and verbalize—or even to think about—their goals in life. They just drift along, take the path of least resistance, and see no need to become any more than they already are.

A girl who thought she was a well-liked person said that she wanted to be the most popular person in the school. She wanted to become "just what I am now. But, I really don't know what my goal in life is. I guess I'm just drifting along hoping for the best and just grabbing what I can reach. I'm afraid to face a goal . . . I'm afraid to face life, without a promise!"

The inability to settle on an occupational identity disturbs many young people. Some of them tend to over-identify with the heroes of cliques and crowds to the point of almost losing all individuality.

What do your young people want to become? Are any of their dreams and goals reflected in the following?

> *Girl.*—I want to become an adult. That sounds weird, but it is true. I want people to think I have some sense. I want to be honest and unashamed of myself and anything I do . . . My main goals in life are to serve God, become a good wife and mother, and be an example to others of complete happiness.

> *Girl.*—I would like to be the kind of person who never hurts others (the kind of person who only shows a feeling of warmth and cheer). I want to contribute only happiness to the world. I want only to benefit the world, not harm it. (She lives with her father.)

> *Girl* (Parents divorced, lives with mother).—I think I want to be an honest, helpful, understanding person, who cares and is involved in economic and political projects. I

want to become a strong person who can shoulder some of the burdens of my friends and one who can flow his emotions into the people who don't care enough. My goals include a husband and some adopted children. My chief purpose, I believe, is to make other people care about world problems and how they can be handled.

Girl.—I guess more than anything, I would like to be opposite of the person I have said I am. I want to improve on my patience, obedience, understanding, more broad-minded, and maybe someday I'll be mature enough to make a good wife.

Boy.—I would like to be a fun-loving Casanova, with the girls always around me and plenty of money, but loved by all. I would like to become a well self-controlled person, receiving everyone's attention. I would like to reach the top in whatever I do. I hate to be second or third.

Boy.—I would like to be a normal American with a job, house, car, and family. I would like to have lots of friends and help people in other countries to have freedom as we in the U.S. do.

Boy.—I would like to be the kind of person that most people are: common. I want to work for what I get and take care of what I get . . . I want to become a person with high morals. When the chips are down I want the energy to come on stronger. I want to have a beautiful wife, a wonderful family, and a nice home. I want to be respected by my fellow citizens, but most of all I want to vote.

Boy.—I would like to become a person that people could look up to and be proud of. I want to go to college and make something out of myself, then get married and have a family.

Boy.—I would like to be a person who is took seriously. I would like to become a serious-minded, well-intentioned individual. My goal is to become as rich and important as I possibly can.

Boy.—I would like to be a person who is kindhearted, very well liked, and a real benefit to the community . . . I also want to have plenty of time to do church work.

Boy.—I would like to be a person that is liked by everyone and that has enough get up and go about him to make something out of himself. I want to become a successful person, yet not so successful that I become one of those stereotyped high society snobs. My main purpose in life is to be a help to someone, and everyone if possible.

Boy.—I would like to be the kind of person everyone likes. Getting along with people also seems important to me . . . I would like to have a normal life in which hard work is essential.

Boy.—I do not want to change in any way, but only to broaden my mind. My goals in life are to get through college and live a decent and respectful life with a good job and a wonderful wife.

FOUR IN ONE

How in the world can a young man or woman bring together these four often-diversified images into a single, unified self-image? How can he narrow the gap between the real self and the ideal self? "A positive attitude toward the self in all aspects of life is a most important determinant of successful life adjustment. The individual's concept of himself is at the core of his thinking, motivation, and behavior. It largely determines how an adolescent perceives his friends, his family, his potential vocation, and other aspects of his life." [8]

When a teen-ager clarifies who he or she is, then other questions are less difficult to answer, as Dr. Duvall points out. "To drink or not to drink, to drive like crazy or with prudence, to exploit others unmercifully or to find satisfaction in service,—these dilemmas are solved only as one can answer the haunting questions—Who am I? What am I going to do with my life?" [9]

The writer of Proverbs said it this way: "For as he thinketh in his heart, so is he" (Prov. 23 :7).

A youth can build self-confidence by engaging in activities and situations where he can succeed. If he cannot succeed, he may resort to self-blame and self-depreciation. He may even try to destroy things or hurt people in the process.

A healthy self-image is not attained overnight. It is a long and difficult process. But each youth must make his own pilgrimage to the land of his *Self*. The path is not straight. It is not smooth. Sometimes he will move forward with strength and courage. At other times he will stumble and fall. He will be proud when he climbs a hill or rounds a curve. He will be distressed when he falls on the rocks. But he is entitled to do his own stumbling, his own falling. He will learn how to stand, and walk, and run freely to the land of his *Self*. The adults who love him will, as Dr. Duvall says, protect him from life's disasters, but not from life's bruises. "For he has a right to learn, to become, to be." [10]

In 1969, the Sunday School Board of the Southern Baptist Convention completed a serious survey of the attitudes and beliefs of Southern Baptist Youth. A synopsis of the survey is contained as Appendix B at the back of this book.

1. J. Phillip Landgrave, *Purpose* (Nashville: Broadman Press, 1969).

2. Gene Usdin, M.D., editor, *Adolescence, Care and Counseling* (Philadelphia: J. B. Lippincott Co., 1967), p. 9.

3. Robert L. Browning, *Communicating With Junior Highs* (Nashville: Methodist Graded Press, 1968), p. 62.

4. Ira J. Gordon, *Human Development: From Birth Through Adolescence* (New York: Harper, 1962), p. 80.

5. John Kord Lagemann, "Self-Fulfilling Prophecy—A Key to Success," *Reader's Digest,* February 1969, p. 80.

6. Stephen J. Goeberg, *The Experience of Adolescence* (Cambridge: Schenkman Publishing Co., 1965), p. 103.

7. *Op. cit.,* Gordon, p. 284.

8. Ruth Strang, *The Adolescent Views Himself* (New York: McGraw-Hill Book Co., Inc., 1957), p. 78.

9. Evelyn M. Duvall, *Today's Teen-agers* (New York: Association Press, 1966), p. 47.

10. *Ibid.,* p. 48.

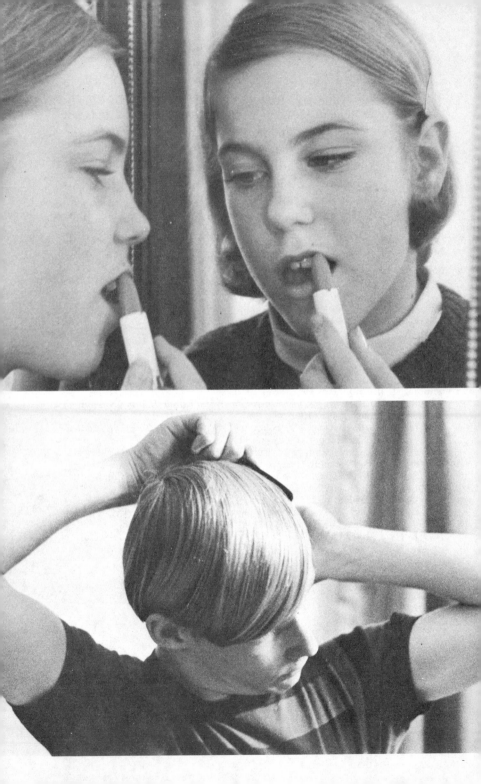

Chapter 2. GROWING UP AND OUT

A few short years
From 12 or 13 on;
Magic years,
Moody years,
Tasting life and food and fun;
Ball game years,
Blue jean years,
Muddled, wild, fumbling years,
Until we die . . .
Until the tomb of 20 opens wide,
Where each of us must lie
Like lost and lifeless butterflies
And then be born again
As old, outdated, adult men.
We live our muddled years
Like a moth against a pane,
Excited by a light
That fills our wings with fierce flight
But cannot set us free
Until we feel insane.[1]

Norman C. Habel

"UNTIL WE FEEL INSANE!" .... Why do youth feel insane? One young girl expressed it this way: When I was fourteen we went back to visit in the town where I spent my childhood. I had not been back for three years. Everywhere we went, everybody we saw (every adult that is) looked at me like I was some monster or something. "My, how you've grown!" ... *What'd they expect? A dwarf?* "I can't believe my eyes!" ... *Heavens, do I look that bad?* "Don't tell me this is little Susie?" *No, lady, I changed into a freak named Murgetroid.* "My, how you've grown, . . . my, how you've grown . . . my, how you've grown . . . grown . . . grown" . . . *Do they want me to stay a baby all my life? Yeh, maybe that is just what they would like me to do. All adults want you to stay a baby all your life, so they can tell you what to eat, what to wear, and how to act. They either want you to stay a baby all your life or else they try to make you feel more insane than you already feel. Sometimes I think I'm just not going to make it. I'm not sure it's worth the effort* . . . "My, how you've grown!"

This young girl had been rather proud of the fact that she had grown up and out in the right places ... Proud, that is, until she heard these comments repeated like a bad phonograph record. She began to think: Am I abnormal or something? Of course, the adults involved were *glad* that she had grown. They didn't consider her abnormal, but she was having so much trouble adjusting to and accepting her changing body that she interpreted their reactions incorrectly.

The boy, too, has to deal with adult comments, maybe about his changing voice. He doesn't even have to go away for two or three years for adults to notice the change. His voice plays tricks on him. He can't trust it. One moment it will come out one way and the next moment it will come out another way. Going through a voice change is bad enough without adults calling attention to it.

The emotional eruptions of youth (the teen-age girl who bursts into tears for no reason at all) cannot be understood apart from some knowledge of the changing physiology of adolescence.

Girls begin growth spurts at an earlier age than boys. Most begin shooting up at about eleven and reach physical maturity at about seventeen. The boy's growth spurt begins one or two years later. There is no one age at which it is normal to develop certain physical characteristics. Every child has an individual pattern of growth unique to him. Duvall expressed it simply and descriptively when she said: "Both early-developing and late-blooming youngsters traverse the same pathway, each at his own rate, like the express train and the slow freight moving over the same track; one may go swiftly to the end of the line while the other starts more slowly, stops more often, and takes more time, yet both trains go over the same route and eventually arrive at the same destination." [2]

At whatever speed the youth develops, his growth process is a beautiful miracle. That miracle is the subject of this chapter.

Estrogens, the female hormone, begin increasing in a girl sometime between eight and eleven years of age to signal the beginning of puberty. The average for the beginning of menstruation is thirteen and a half, but the normal limits stretch from about ten to sixteen.

The development of secondary sex characteristics in both male and female, "mark the beginning of sexual maturation." [3] Obviously, the physical sexual development of youth coincides with social development. This social development, which includes dating and the selection of a marriage partner, is of crucial importance. The subject is treated in Appendix A of this book.

Probably the most striking nonsexual physiological change appearing at the time of puberty is the sudden decline in basal metabolism.

The heart almost doubles in size during adolescence. There is also an accelerated rate of growth of the lungs, especially for boys.

Marked changes take place in the structure of the skin and the skin glands. The delicate skin of childhood gives way to a coarser skin. Pores become enlarged and the sweat glands increasingly active. Oil-producing glands of the skin increase in size and activity and are closely associated with the common skin disturbances during adolescence. The glands develop more rapidly than the ducts and the ducts frequently become plugged. Then the dried oil in the ducts comes in contact with air and oxidation produces the villain, the "blackhead."

Acne, a major skin problem during adolescence, may be caused by an excess of male hormones or by the oil-producing glands in relationship with the disproportionately small hairs.

There is frequently a relationship between emotional upsets and acne. For example, a boy may have a bad case of acne after a violent argument with his father or some other emotional episode in the home. The chemical imbalance (extra adrenalin) resulting from the upset seems to furnish an overstimulation of the oily gland of the skin. An outbreak of rage or hate is often followed with an outbreak of pimples.

The boy especially is concerned about acne, body odors, and what he calls "nervous perspiration." So it seems that the tiny pores and oil glands can cause many problems during the early and middle adolescent years.

The stomach increases in size and capacity. Many mothers begin to believe that their son's stomachs are developing into bottomless pits. Muscular strength lags behind growth in height and weight.

Increase in physical activity may be caused by secretion of the thyroid gland. This secretion adds to their restlessness, resulting in a desire to be on the go 'til all hours at the very time they need more sleep than usual.

The voice change is one of the most obvious outward changes in the adolescent boy's body. It becomes lower in pitch and more resonant. The boy's "Adam's apple" becomes enlarged and the vocal cords within it increase to approximately twice their former length. This change results in the voice dropping approximately an octave in pitch. The girl's voice also changes, but it does so at a much slower rate and is more a change in texture than in pitch. Contrary to what many youth or adults may believe, voice change is not a good indicator of the extent of sexual development.

How Does Youth Take All of This?

There is some question whether or not the normal stability of body function is disrupted by all the changes which occur during adolescence. If the body function is disrupted, some of the teen-ager's behavior can be attributed to the state of his internal environment, since the body has to learn and establish new patterns and rhythms. It is a simple task for the preadolescent to sit down to a table. In adolescence, this same process may cause havoc. He may knock things flying when he didn't mean to. He may kick a chair in a classroom when he had absolutely no intention of doing so. He may be so embarrassed after accidentally knocking or kicking things that he covers up for it by pretending that his action was intentional.

Adding to the confusion is the fact that the growth of different organ systems and body parts do not keep pace with each other. Until he becomes accustomed to his body as a sexually mature organism, he is plagued and embarrassed by new and unfamiliar experiences.[4]

Also disturbing to the boys is the "fat period" which occurs near the beginning of the growth spurt. Overweight boys and girls get laughed at and called names. In order to survive, they may shrug off this teasing as though they do not care, but most often it is as painful as a dagger thrust.

There will always be individuals who mature much earlier or much later than most of their classmates. Each individual, to be sure, follows his own unique pattern of physical-emotional-mental-social development; and yet, there are some who develop so early or so late that they have problems accepting their rates of growth. The boys' shower room and locker room in the junior high school gym can be a place for either exhibitionism or intense embarrassment. Each boy becomes aware of whether he fits the other guy's image of the male physique. He may become the object of ridicule if his physical appearance has small boy or feminine characteristics, or if he has not yet attained to physical maturity.

Quite often, small boys try to conceal their insecure feelings about their sizes by becoming loud-mouths or show-offs.

Adolescent girls worry about their skin and their weight. Girls do not escape the acne syndrome either. This problem is especially worrisome during the last few days before the menstrual period begins, because of the apparent connection between hormone output and skin glands.

Strang states that there are six problems connected with the adolescent's accepting and making the most of his physical capacities: (1) being overweight or underweight; (2) not getting enough sleep; (3) having a poor complexion or skin trouble; (4) smoking and drinking; (5) having trouble with teeth or eyes; (6) being nervous.[5]

The changing body affects the youth's attitudes, while attitudes toward his changing body affects his image of himself. A big, overgrown boy may act like a bully. An early-developed girl may feel pushed outside her peer group, especially if she is approached by boys outside her age group. The late-developing girl may feel that she is treated almost like a freak by the other girls. In fact, her fears may be realized.

When a youth feels completely adequate physically (and few of them do), he or she may tend to neglect other aspects of development. When he feels extremely inadequate physically, he may try harder in other areas to please the adults in his life— his teachers (at school and church), parents, friends—in order to build up his self-confidence. The danger with such a response is that adult teachers or parents may take advantage of this seemingly good, obedient child who shows respect and fail to realize that he is simply craving acceptance and praise so badly that he will even take it from an adult . . . that is, until he can build up enough self-confidence to relate to his peers.

The excessive rate of physical growth tends toward excessives in other areas: excessive strength, which prompts the boy to show off his physical prowess in weight lifting and strenuous sports; excessive eating habits, the "I can eat more hamburgers than you" kind; excessive activism—he can't stay still, always on the go; and excessive enthusiasm for things he likes—stays up all night (even studying) just to prove that his body can take it. In middle and late adolescence, the young person feels that at long last he can count on his body to perform in certain predictable ways. He thinks he possesses unlimited energy, so he tests his bodily limits by sports; staying up late; and using alcoholic beverages, tobacco, sex, and dope. He has passed through a period when he could not count on his body. Now he seeks to find out just how much that body can take.

There is no escaping the fact that the period called adolescence is one of great physical change and strain. Nevertheless, most young people move through it quite nicely. Garrison reminds us that for some, "physical change can present real physiological and psychological problems. These adolescents will need the help and understanding of mature adults." [6]

This is one task of workers with youth!

---

1. Norman C. Habel, *Wait A Minute, Moses* (St. Louis: Concordia Publishing Co., 1965), p. 14.

2. Evelyn M. Duvall, *Today's Teen-agers* (New York: Association Press, 1966), p. 44.

3. Ruth Strang, *The Adolescent Views Himself* (New York: McGraw-Hill Book Co., 1957), p. 23.

4. Ira J. Gordon, *Human Development: From Birth Through Adolescence* (New York: Harper, 1962), p. 340.

5. *Op. cit.*, Strang, p. 201.

6. James F. Adams, *Understanding Adolescence* (Boston: Allyn and Bacon, Inc., 1968), p. 65.

Chapter 3. FEELING GROOVY

EMOTIONS ARE EVASIVE; they are hard to define, or even to describe. "I feel like . . ." How does a person "feel"? How does he *tell* another how he feels?

The area of emotional development is a tricky one to explore. For the nonprofessional, the study is elusive and difficult to deal with. Feelings reflect each individual's attitudes toward himself, toward others, and toward life. Interpersonal relationships contribute to the feeling of security or insecurity of the individual.

Adolescent emotional development is especially hard for the adult to comprehend. The adult has experienced the emotional gamut and (hopefully) has become stabilized into basic patterns of emotional response. It is hard for him to remember his floundering attempts to relate to people—the times when he felt totally unloved, unwanted, rejected, defeated. Therefore, it is hard for the adult to empathize with the adolescent. He may even look lightly upon youth's intense feelings or pass them off as disrespect. The adolescent usually responds to this attitude with a verbal, "You don't care how I feel."

As pleasant as the quiet, peaceful, obedient, passive adolescent is to be around, most adult workers and parents know that emotion must be expressed—that the withdrawn, afraid-to-speak person who is harboring fear or hostility, or both, is really in trouble.

All of us, adults and youth alike, share a common humanity. Whether we are rich or poor, well-bred or ill-bred, educated or not educated, white or black; whether we speak English or not; whether we live by the acceptable codes of morality or not; whether we are disciples of Christ or not—we all still share a common humanity. Jesus not only identified with man, *he was man.* And behold! it was very good! If being human, then, is good, it is unhealthy for any person to deny his humanity. Likewise, no attempt should be made to try to force youth to deny their humanity. The authors' oldest daughter expressed her feeling for life in a poem:

BEING

Loneliness comes gently
Invading my being, becoming myself.
Its silent irruption is like a phantasma;
I cannot believe this hideous dream.
It is just a dream?
(Please tell me it is.)
I cannot live to love by myself,
For that is not life, that is not love.
I sit in the middle; the circle of life
revolves around me—
its full empathy
Resounds in my soul.

Kaleidoscopes of
flashing brilliant
lights and faces,
all who mirror
Suffering, hate, confusion,
prejudice, apathy,
or maybe
Death.

Prismatic dreams, desultory thoughts
Of life, perhaps no thoughts at all.
They come to me, each his kind
Invade my soul and blow my mind.
    idiot—rejected
    bigot—defeated
    black man—hated
    rebel—misjudged
    stereotype—misunderstood
    loss leader—unloved
    hypocrite—alone
    Christ—outcast
        God! Hell is murky!
Yes they say again
Je ne vaux rien.
        Tell me it's not true!
"Life's but a walking shadow,"
Or so the poets tell us.
Muffled drums induction to hell's filth and starkness,
Hate's consuming fires,
Hell's own destruction, hot breath of darkness
Fans the funeral pyres.
             —Brenda Murphree

Adolescent emotional storms are as changeable and as unpredictable as the weather. Adult response to the ebb and flow of the flood waters has a definite effect upon that ebb and flow. Dr. Reuben S. Roy says that the emotional accompaniments of the adolescent are less clearly understood even by many who work' regularly with them than any other phase of adolescent development. This fact can be explained, he maintains, "by the truism that many of the observable behaviorisms of the adolescent—his flagrant bad manners, his emotional unpredictability, his seclusiveness, his clannishness, his difficulty in communicating with his elders—are not clear reflections of his real person: they are the heat and smoke of the process of growth." [1]

The goal of growth is what we often call maturity. Lofton Hudson says that "maturity is not primarily a matter of mind; it is more of the emotions. You may have a very bright mind and yet, emotionally, be filled with prejudices, ill will, bad temper, self-pity, sensitiveness, and irresponsibility." [2]

In dealing with adolescent emotion, the first essential is to understand the individual. Individuals perceive their basic needs in different ways. "What constitutes security for one person is not security for another. Approval by a teacher may be just the thing an adolescent does not want; parental affection may make it more difficult for him to gain adult independence." [3] Some teens do not accept certain adults for fear that they will be rejected by their age-mates. "Each individual copes with the environment as he perceives it and as he experiences it at a given instant. Failure to cope with the environment as perceived causes emotional stress and tension." [4]

Why This Feeling of Insecurity?

> I feel that most people do not like me. Some people say that I am conceited, but I try not to be. Secondly, I am forever in fear that my sister will tell my mother that I don't eat lunch. Fortunately, we do not have lunch together, but she always finds out. To others my worries may seem trivial, but to me they are not.

This fourteen-year-old girl wants to be taken seriously. Her worries are not trivial to her. A fifteen-year-old girl expressed her worries like this:

> My worry of losing weight goes with the worry of meeting new people. One reason I dislike the idea of meeting someone is that I am afraid he will not like me. Then the idea of driving worries me because I have never driven before, but I am going to try to conquer this worry by taking driver's education.

A fifteen-year-old girl said: "On the more personal side (my worries) are finding a boyfriend and eating too much. Probably these affect each other. I'll have to solve these problems myself."

Note the fears listed by these three girls: fear of the unknown; meeting new people and learning to drive; fear of acceptance; concern with weight problems; and fear of parental disapproval.

Excessive attention to clothes on the part of the boy and make-up and clothes on the part of the girl usually indicate a lack of self-acceptance. On the other hand, extreme neglect of personal appearance may indicate self-rejection.

How many times have you heard, "But I know they were talking about me when I walked up." Or, "Everybody thinks I'm a freak or something with my hair cut this way. No decent boy wears his hair like this. It just means that *everybody* [there's that word again] will know you still treat me like a baby—telling me how to get my hair cut."

Dr. David Elkind, Professor of Psychology at the University of Rochester, said that "when he is in social situations, the adolescent feels as if he is on stage, and that everyone is watching and evaluating his behavior. He is thus constantly performing for an audience which is, in part at least, of his own making. It is this feeling that others are as concerned with him as he is with himself that is the substance of adolescent *egocentrism*." [5]

Loved or Bound?

A part of the adolescent's feelings of insecurity comes from feeling unloved by his parents. He may be loved without *feeling* loved. But then, he does not want to be bound to this love exclusively. In fact, he does not want to be bound, period. Thus, the turmoil involved in emancipation results from the youth trying to learn how to move away from a dominated existence. For parents to continually point out his faults, correct his mistakes and order or forbid him to behave in certain ways humiliates him, decreases his self-esteem, and undermines his self-confidence. It may cause him to believe that he does not have what it takes to become an acceptable adult. "Children and young people tend to feel toward themselves as other people who are significant in their lives feel toward them." [6]

The path of self-understanding and self-realization is never a smooth one. There surely will be some rough spots. The youth is going to drop the ball a few times. Fumbling is inevitable. "The impulse to self-assertion competes with the instinct to resist change; the individual sets up defenses to preserve his present idea of himself. He rationalizes. He resists the impact of thoughts that would make it necessary for him to reexamine his self-concept. Growth in self-understanding implies a search, a struggle, a continual endeavor. It is a process, rather than an end result." [7]

The adolescent needs to feel confident in his own abilities. The child who feels secure in his parents' love is more likely to gain this confidence. The child who feels secure in his parents' love is more likely to be successful in making and keeping friends. He has faith in his parents. He can learn to have faith in friends. He trusts his parents. He can learn to trust his friends. One who feels loved is more able to express love in healthy ways.

The Pendulum Swings

The emotional barometer of youth soars and plummets—high as a kite one minute, low as a heavy anchor the next; soaring like a bird today, dragging like an iron ball tomorrow. *Normal* adolescence is marked by *extremes* in behavior and emotion.

Most parents and workers with youth have accepted youth's up and down moods as part of the stabilization process. It is interesting to note how the youth sees himself in this respect.

A high school senior girl described her feelings like this:

> I am a complex person and hard to understand. I am often moody and withdrawn into a shell. Sometimes I become too demanding, or I may be too stingy. I live in both a realistic and a dream world. I wish to accomplish many things in my life. I feel many things with strong emotion. But I have many doubts.

Another youth expressed herself this way:

> I suppose mixed-up would best describe me . . . I know I am unsure, but sometimes I'm a little too happy-go-lucky. I

enjoy people and . . . I enjoy staying alone by myself at home . . . Understanding what's really happening is hard for me, because everything seems mixed up.

A sixteen-year-old girl whose parents were divorced evaluated herself and her emotional extremes:

> I am often a selfish, inconsiderate person who would rather play games than face reality. I complain much too often and feel conceited at the most inopportune times. Then, sometimes I am quiet, while I am contemplating some soul-searching questions and solutions.

In testing programs, moodiness is no longer mentioned by the adolescent himself as being a common characteristic, although it is generally considered by the authorities to be a definite part of the growing up experience. Youth may recognize their extremes in moods and just not want to tell about them. Or, they may not recognize them. Or, it may be that they are such ordinary daily occurrences that they do not seem worth mentioning.[8]

Nevertheless, the pendulum swings freely from moods of depression to elation, passing through the less extreme emotional ones.

Perhaps workers should let them know in natural, normal learning experiences that they understand and experience feelings of love and hate—that it is all a matter of degree—that even the process of learning to cope with these emotions is a continuing one, successful with adults only by degree.

---

1. Gene Usdin, M.D., editor, *Adolescence: Care and Counseling* (Philadelphia: J. B. Lippincott Co., 1967), p. 17.
2. R. Lofton Hudson, *The Religion of a Mature Person* (Nashville: Broadman Press, 1952), p. 2.
3. Ruth Strang, *The Adolescent Views Himself* (New York: McGraw-Hill Book Co., 1957), p. 475.
4. *Ibid.*, p. 475.
5. James F. Adams, editor, *Understanding Adolescence* (Boston: Allyn and Bacon, Inc., 1968), p. 153.
6. *Op. cit.*, Strang, p. 116.
7. *Ibid.*, p. 82.
8. *Ibid.*, p. 150.

Chapter 4. HE'S GOT A MIND OF HIS OWN

PERHAPS L. L. Day displayed a slight "tongue-in-cheek" air when he wrote, "Sad to say that, after the age of eighteen, we slough off millions (or maybe it's billions) of brain cells every day. And that these cells are never replaced. Naturally, this process escalates as we grow older. So that by the time we reach middle age we are down to our last trillion." [1] So far as we know at this time, one will never have any more brainpower than he has as a youth. Studies by Jones and Conrad in 1933 provide a basis for concluding that mental growth increases rapidly and reaches a peak at about sixteen years of age; after which the rate of growth slows considerably. However, persons in school continue to progress in mental growth until at least twenty years of age. Later studies indicate that mental progress slows during adulthood due to lack of exercise in the various fields of study. However, the imagination is most active between the ages of nineteen and thirty-five.[2]

Foundations for brainpower must include: personal responsibility for one's own learning, group-centered learning processes, and freedom of individual initiative and investigation. These contemporary educational principles must not be violated. To do so is to hinder learning and mental development.

The Development of Brainpower

A tremendous amount of progress in mental ability takes place between the ages of twelve and fifteen. Various levels throughout the development of this ability are of extreme importance to the worker with Youth. Leaders will work with younger Youth in quite different ways than they would with older Youth.

The following list defines some specific areas of mental development. These areas should be studied by the reader with the view to identify the general level of the group with which he works. In the case of those working with Youth of the entire span of years, the levels should still be noted so as to avoid the mistake of relating to each age level in the same way.

1. YOUTH ARE DEVELOPING THE ABILITY TO THINK ABSTRACTLY AND TO LEARN HIGHLY DIFFICULT MATERIAL.

The elementary school student and the college student are quite far apart in their abilities to think abstractly. The twelve through seventeen age range is the period during which the obvious development takes place.

When a twelve-year-old (or seventh grader) comes into the Youth department, he still has not developed the ability to think abstractly. He intensely *wants* to be a teen-ager, but he is not one. He still thinks in *concrete,* rather than in *abstract* terms. He can learn *facts,* but he has a difficult time reasoning. His application of divine truth is in specifics. He is not able to digest facts and apply them independently to his life. He thinks of forgiveness in terms of persons, not as a concept. He thinks of salvation in terms of places and people, not in terms of discipleship. He responds to a call to missions on the basis of concrete facts or events about a nation or people, not because of a view of widening the kingdom's influence. This concrete thinking does not make him less religious than high school Youth, but does call attention to the need to lead him in ways he can understand.

In different speeds of development, Youth pass through the thirteenth and fourteenth years to the fifteenth. Some of them begin understanding some abstract truths during their thirteenth year. Most do not. Generally, by the age of fifteen, the Youth has developed his mental capacity sufficiently to grapple with doctrinal concepts. Note, however, that he does not automatically start relating the facts he has learned in previous years in Sunday School to a philosophy of life. He is only *capable* of doing so, and the worker with Youth has the opportunity to lead him to do so.

2. YOUTH ARE DEVELOPING THE ABILITY TO EXERCISE CREATIVE IMAGINATION AND INVENTIVENESS.

Youth are creative at all age levels. Indeed, creativity is apparent during all of the childhood levels also. Creativity, however, becomes more sophisticated with each passing year.

A twelve- or thirteen-year-old is creative generally within certain defined boundaries. Older Youth are usually able to establish their own boundaries. For example, a younger Youth would have difficulty doing a collage when given only the general instruction, "Do a collage on the Bible." However, if he were instructed to do a collage which shows what the Bible teaches about getting along with people, he would be able to express himself quite creatively.

The same progress is apparent in every creative activity. Consequently, a worker should give sufficient guidance to younger Youth to give them direction. With the fourteen to fifteen age group, less direction is necessary, and with sixteen- to seventeen-year-olds, they're competent to plan activities or express themselves creatively in other ways with much less supervision.

This difference in ability to respond to creative activities accounts for some of the frustration workers with Youth must face. The worker who does not seek to define the potential response of his Youth will likely either use activities which seem childish to the younger Youth (a very sore point to him) or use activities beyond his capability. When the ability is understood, though, the creativity of Youth at any age level is surprising even to the professional Youth worker.

Learning to think requires both opportunity and practice. Using one's mind constructively is not an automatic response. It is not accomplished by routine exercises in sameness. "Young minds must have stimulation . . . if they are to grow; and young people must have a chance to develop and test their intellectual skills." [3]

The mind must be liberated from confinements in the past before it can make new discoveries in ideas, principles, facts, and planned experiences. The mind needs practice in dealing with the present and the future—not with the past only. Edgar Dale stated the point strongly and plainly, "A good mind does not reinvent the alphabet or the wheel. It starts its hard work where others left off." He continues with a harsh reprimand of some educational systems and processes: "Unfortunately, schools and colleges tend to value memory more highly than creativity, passive reception over thoughtful analysis, ready-made answers over searching questions. There is a danger that students will be so busy attending classes that they don't have time left to get an education." [4] Leaders in churches and parents of Youth should consider whether these same charges could be leveled at some of the programs and activities which are planned for Youth. Often, classes and activities are geared toward rote memorization rather than toward understanding. The 1969 study of Southern Baptist Youth showed that they were rather proficient in answering doctrinal questions accurately but scored poorly on questions designed to show application of doctrinal meanings to life. (See Appendix B.)

3. YOUTH ARE DEVELOPING THE ABILITY TO THINK INDEPENDENTLY, TO QUESTION THE STATUS QUO.

This developing mental ability is apparent in the conflict between the younger Youth and his parents and other adults.

Tension is created as the Youth challenges the value of a church or parental concept for his own life. Rules are no longer acceptable on authority only. As the Youth becomes more mature, he expects rules to be supportable with reasons—and the reasons must be contemporary in application.

Again, the development is progressive over the twelve to seventeen age period. The early adolescent reacts toward persons and personal habits. As he grows, he reacts to ideas with increasing ability.

4. THEY CAN PLAN A LONG-RANGE COURSE OF ACTION.

This ability is related to creativity and to the ability (No. 8) to conceptualize time. All Youth are concerned with and relate to immediate events. They live largely from event to event. As they mature, though, their horizons broaden. They become increasingly concerned with vocational choices and become better able to visualize the time required for preparation. Marriage is understood as a possibility within the foreseeable future by the older Youth; whereas to younger Youth, that marriage is so far away as to be another world. Since the younger male Youth is so related to *now* and marriage is so distant, his curiosity about sex is pretty consuming. (See Appendix A.)

The ability of various age levels to plan should be of major consideration in working with Youth, so that activities and preparation for them will be challenging, while not beyond their abilities to perform.

5. THEY ARE DEVELOPING THE ABILITY TO GIVE LONG AND INTENSE ATTENTION TO MATTERS IN WHICH THEY ARE INTERESTED, AND THEY BECOME INCREASINGLY READY TO WORK HARD FOR A SENSE OF ACHIEVEMENT AND TO REACH CHOSEN GOALS, BOTH IMMEDIATE AND DISTANT.

The attention span of younger Youth is shorter than that of older Youth—more nearly like an older child. Consequently, a worker should plan for those activities which require concentration to be of relatively short duration. Also, a special study should be contained in as short a time period as possible. For example, a weekend retreat would result in a better learning atmosphere than would be possible with similar material and plans over a period of weeks.

Older Youth are better able to handle learning activities which are segmented and separated by time. However, since all Youth relate best to single events, activities which are capsuled in a short time allotment have advantages for successful outcomes.

In activities in which curriculum is used, short units of study —three or four weeks at most—are most likely to be valid learning experiences. Older Youth can handle longer units of study.

6. THEY CAN USE THEIR READING SKILLS EFFECTIVELY.

Vocabulary, both in terms of the choice and the use of words in conversation, is an excellent index to mental development. The use of large, unusual, or technical words and expressions is not in itself proof of intelligence; but, a deliberate and appropriate choice of words is evidence of healthy reasoning powers.

One of the most effective means of developing vocabulary is through a hobby which requires broadened experiences and mental exercise. Motors, collections, sports, travel, arts, creative and expressional activities, plus the research related to such hobbies, can be very valuable for increasing mental faculties.

Naturally, the abilities of Youth to read more difficult material develops over the age span. In selecting materials to be read before a group or on which a Youth can base a report, the content should be carefully evaluated. Many poems and profound, well-written prose are too abstract for younger Youth to understand, even though the vocabulary of the piece may be simple.

7. THEY ARE DEVELOPING THEIR ABILITIES TO DO CREATIVE WORK
   IN FIELDS RELATED TO THEIR TALENTS AND INTERESTS.

One of the significant accomplishments of the Youth years is that of the young person coming to understand his abilities and interests. He explores various avenues of expressions, various subjects, and various ways to relate to people.

Each Youth needs reflection time when he can be detached from others. He needs to focus his mind inward upon himself and those matters which seem important to him at the moment, especially as they reflect his relationships with his special friends. Mental energy focused inward is normal and healthy, provided it does not become a frequent exercise in moodiness and depression as a way of life. Times of aloneness are often necessary and healthy for assimilation of social and esthetic experiences into the total fabric of life.

The worker with younger Youth can aid them in making their choices by opening as many doors to exploration as possible. Activities and learning experiences which give opportunities for any Youth to test himself on some ability, interest, or interpersonal relationship make possible his development in many areas. Part-time and summer jobs can be very valuable for testing and developing abilities and interests. As he matures, the Youth will discard experiences which he has found unsatisfactory.

Older Youth, while they have not explored all of their potentials, will have settled on a number of interests and discarded others. The worker who provides a choice of ways to do creative work in fields of a Youth's interest will be allowing him to relate the church to his life.

8. THEY ARE LEARNING TO CONCEPTUALIZE TIME AND SPACE.

When a pre-teen is promoted to a Youth department, he has already accumulated a considerable number of facts, Bible stories, and information on various church-related subjects. However, he has not yet arranged all of his knowledge in chronological order. He may be able to tell the story of a Bible character, for example, but may not know whether the person lived before or after Christ. During Youth years, a person learns to identify his knowledge chronologically and to arrange it in an orderly fashion. Distance has also become more meaningful to him. He learns the relationship between time and space.

Inner personal problems of Youth and the perplexing problems in society deserve great attention by workers, since highly developed young minds will affect present circumstances. More significantly, they will shape the future of national and world cultural, religious, and political systems. Workers must prod Youth to think realistically and toward the future—in order to assume personal responsibility for shaping the future. W. C. Fields pierces complacency at this point. He says, "Our entire educational system, including that fostered by the churches, looks backward, not forward. We have many courses in history but none in 'future.' We must explore the possibilities of tomorrow quite as systematically as we now study about Rome, the Magna Charta, the American Revolution, William Carey, Annie Armstrong, and the record of Christian missions." [5]

9. THEY ARE DEVELOPING THE ABILITY TO GRAPPLE
   WITH MORAL AND ETHICAL CONCEPTS AND TO EXPLORE
   MANY A VARIETY OF SUBJECT AREAS.

By the fifteenth or sixteenth year, Youth are able to handle abstract truths fairly well. Some of them will be rather sophisticated by this age.

The grappling of Youth with moral and ethical concepts does not infer altogether that they are rebelling against the traditional. To be sure, they challenge the *status quo*, but they often arrive at moral codes which are acceptable by Christian standards when allowed to express themselves. Generally, they are more idealistic than are adults—partly because of immaturity, partly because they apply truths with devastating consistency.

If Youth are not allowed to express their feelings about moral codes and ethical standards, their development into mature Christians will be seriously hampered. An atmosphere in which a Youth can express his doubts freely will aid him in exploring the value of Christian teaching to his life.

A thorough understanding of Christian teachings comes

about through studying a subject from various directions. By the sixteenth or seventeenth year, a wide variety of approaches is possible. Missions can be studied, for example, through Bible passages, doctrine, geography, social ethics, history, or methods—to list only a few approaches.

Edgar Dale, editor of *The News Letter,* Ohio State University Bureau of Research, illustrates the necessity for continuing mental experiences as he tells of seeing a pile of secondhand dictionaries in a college book store. He states that students had passed their English courses but had not learned the values and methods of using their dictionaries and therefore sold them. The question relates to church workers: Are church Youth learning the values and proper use of the Bible in church-related experiences? Are they helped to discover and use translations in current language? Are their lives becoming stronger and richer as a result of their studies? One main sign of effective religious education is the capacity for thinking critically and creatively. This thinking must be based on valid biblical principles, with results shared through speech, attitude, actions, and quality of inner life.

Attitudes and Brainpower

One of the most effective factors involved in the education of a young person is his own attitude toward learning and the probable uses he will make of his learning.

Inner motivation is a necessary ally to mental growth and maturity. "Even though one is hemmed in by a rigid pattern of life, there is a possibility of progress as long as one retains the capacity to learn." [6]

Church leaders do well when they encourage and help adolescents to develop and use their minds during peak years of mental capacity. The personal and group values of highly developed minds are becoming greater, not less. The view of one leading educator is that "In the late 1970's or early 1980's, it is not unlikely that students will graduate from high school with knowledge and social insights equal to or superior to that of a person who earned a bachelor's degree in the 1960's." [7] Church leaders who do not respect this superiority may drive the most capable and promising Youth out of the Church.

Harnessing the Brainpower

Leaders and parents alike should realize that there are many factors to be taken into account in relation to mental development. The Youth's environment is, or can in most cases be, flexible and changeable. He is affected by these changes, many of which he cannot choose for himself. A family's move to a different city or area, the attitudes of a Youth's group of friends, interest of a teacher who succeeds in sparking his intellect, reaction against the teacher, church experiences, and attitudes of brothers and sisters are only a few of the obvious influences on Youth. Furthermore, mental functions undergo considerable alterations as one grows into and through adolescence. "Abstract thinking ability somewhat replaces concrete, static, hard and direct ways of thinking and dealing with things and experiences . . . he can deal with ideas, theories, symbols, and symbolic words, concepts, reasoning processes, expressions, pictures, . . . can interpret pictures, cartoons, et cetera, and can discover motives and attitudes and feelings portrayed." [8] He becomes unresponsive to Bible stories and wants to become involved in interpretations and applications.

One of the major changes occurring in educational processes is toward *listening to* Youth instead of merely *talking at* Youth. Learning is truly becoming a two-way street.

An interesting sidelight has been discovered relative to the old theory that girls are smarter than boys as an explanation for differences in their mental activities. One source reveals that "boys show more intellectual energy and more daring than the girls. Girls tend to fill every available line with neat, careful, well-punctuated sentences; boys are likelier to make a flying leap at the subject, pummeling it vigorously in one lively, untidy paragraph." [9] Neither sex, therefore, has prior claim to superiority in brainpower.

Now, admittedly, it might be easier to concentrate on helping young people make comfortable adjustments to life and conditions as we know and understand them than to bother with various approaches to ideas and situations. But isn't it much more realistic, challenging, and exciting to try to become inventive! Creative! Even willing for Youth to surpass adults in every area of achievement! Elson Caldwell has written very appropriately to this point: "As educators turn a speculative eye on the next decade, we must seek to answer questions that most of them have hesitated to face. For what kind of world should we strive to prepare children and youth who will spend most of their lives in the next century? We say this question is crucial because educational policy decisions in the 70's will not only anticipate tomorrow, they probably will help create it." [10] Isn't this as true and timely in religious education as in public education?

Mental development pertains to all areas of life. It is much more than passing exams and getting credit for courses of study. Knowledge must be systematized in order to be useful. This systematizing develops a Youth's philosophy of life. The intellectual values and distinctions which relate to him and his world around him reveal his mental progress toward maturity.

Examples of Brainpower Are Needed

Some adolescents look for signs or examples of mental maturity and continuing development in their parents and church leaders. They are affected by what they observe. Some get the impression that most church leaders allow no room for significant thinking processes in the church. They may even make comparisons with non-church subjects and wonder whether brains are excluded from church.

A specific illustration of the problem in Sunday School, however, is rather sharply described by Mancil Ezell and Josephine Pile: "A teacher may have difficulty in teaching because the Sunday morning schedule of the department is set up for everything but teaching the biblical revelation. It is sometimes planned for assembling, for collecting attendance statistics and offerings, or handing out materials, for miscellaneous speakers and films, for promotional speeches by representatives of the church-wide program, for robing the Youth Choir, and on and on." [11]

Leaders could well set themselves the goal of clearing away the clutter of activities and needless noise which work against mental as well as spiritual growth.

Workers with Youth are obliged to help each Youth accept himself with his own mental capacities and also help him make the best possible use of his mind. There are some who have normal intelligence, but aren't sure of their intellectual potentials as yet. They need help in attaining a healthy self-respect. Some function well below the level of their abilities, due to faulty mental processes or a marked lack of confidence and self-esteem.

1. L. L. Day, editor-at-large, *Saturday Review*, February 22, 1969, p. 3.
2. James F. Adams, editor, *Understanding Adolescence* (Boston: Allyn and Bacon, Inc., 1968), p. 235.
3. Rowena Ferguson, *The Church's Ministry with Senior Highs* (Nashville: Methodist Graded Press, 1968), p. 17.
4. *The News Letter*, Edgar Dale, editor, Ohio State University Bureau of Research, April, 1968.
5. W. C. Fields, *Trumpets in Dixie* (Atlanta: Home Mission Board of the Southern Baptist Convention, 1967), p. 49.
6. Ruth Strang, *The Adolescent Views Himself* (New York: McGraw-Hill Book Co., 1957), p. 18.
7. Harold G. Shane, "Forecast for the 70's Distilled from More Than 400 Books and Articles," *The Journal of the NEA*, January, 1969, p. 31.
8. *Op. cit.*, Fields, pp. 143, 151.
9. *New Republic*, May 20, 1967, p. 12.
10. *Op. cit.*, Shane, p. 32.
11. A. V. Washburn, compiler, *The Sunday School at Work—1968-69, Intermediate Workers' Edition* (Nashville: Convention Press, 1968), p. 85.

PART 2

Youth Learning to Relate

Adaptation to the circumstances of life
and the world around him is a central
task of the adolescent"
— *Carl P. Adatto*

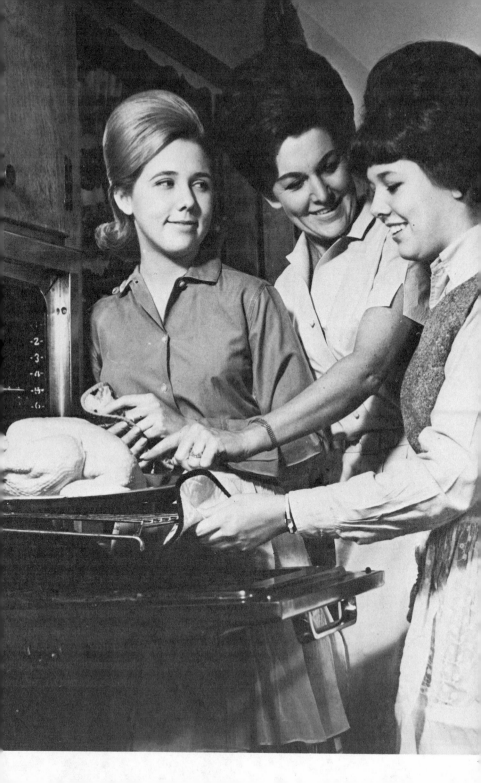

Chapter 5. EVERYONE'S GOTTA HAVE A HOME

DAVID AND VIRGINIA EDENS have written an excellent book entitled, *God Gave Children Parents*. Perhaps some Youth would challenge such a source for parents! But from heaven or not, like it or not, Youth do have parents or parent substitutes. Everyone's gotta have a home!

Studies point to the fact that parents are the single most influential factor in an individual's development. The home provides the main source of love, recognition, reassurance and security, or the lack of it, all of which are so important to Youth. The Youth who does not find emotional security at home will turn to the youth culture exclusively for security and satisfaction.

If his parents are genuinely affectionate, the young person learns to love and be loved. When family members work, play, and make decisions together a self-confident adolescent usually emerges. Adolescents who grow up in homes where there is continual dissension, suspicion, and fault-finding have difficulty finding themselves and establishing themselves in desirable peer groups. Youth often escape from such homes even if they must walk the streets or join a gang.

The Youth who fails to experience acceptance in the family community extends this alienation outside the family. The reverse is also true. If he is successful in establishing a relationship of acceptance and love with his parents, he can extend this acceptance to his peers. "The in-group will be expanded to include others. This is a psychological health maturation process. Psychiatry tells us that one of the marked characteristics of people who enjoy vigorous psychological health is that they do not see many people as strangers." [1] On the other hand, neurotic persons maintain a fixed attitude of fear and hostility by refusing to accept or to learn to know those around them as persons.

The Emancipation Proclamation

When a child is young, it is important for him to see his parents as virtually omnipotent. He needs this assurance for his own protection. Faith in one's parent leads to faith in self. The child also needs to feel a sense of faith and trust in the family structure. As he develops self-sufficiency, though, he has less need for this unreal, fantasy image of the parent as perfect.

Most parents want their children to grow up and accept them as real flesh and blood persons—imperfect, yet loving and caring. They want each child to become independent and emancipated; but the rub comes in *how, how much,* and *when* the emancipation should occur. Many parents intellectually accept the theory that their Youth must become independent of them before he can relate to society as a unique personality. However, they often want him to remain dependent and somewhat subservient to their wishes. The child wants to be treated as an adult, yet often acts in childish, dependent ways. Conflicts often occur when the Youth feels that he needs his parents help on a particular occasion when his parents feel he should exercise self-reliance.

Finding a balance in the dependence-independence role for

parents and Youth is no easy task, yet it is one that must be attempted. The adolescent must develop inner controls. He cannot safely give up the external control of the parent until he has developed within himself the controls or morality to function in a modern society.

Ideally, the Youth will establish a *new* and positive relationship with his parents. He can no longer hold on to relationships as they were when he was a child—even though these experiences had meaning for him then. He is alive *now*. He wants adults to relate to him as he is *now*. He does not want his parents to relate to him on the basis of all the mistakes he made as a child. He wants to forget these mistakes, and relate to his parents, in a more mature way.

Most parents find it a very difficult task to walk the tight rope between helping the Youth when he asks for it and "helping" him constantly whether he asks for it or not. It is almost inevitable that the separating of parent and child is accompanied by a turmoil in which both parents and Youth feel disappointed or hurt.

"Goodby to Oedipus" was the title of an article which appeared in 1959, but the mother's advice to herself about her son is still very sound.

> For me and mine, the end of the idyll is very much in view. He is on the turn now, like milk just ready to curdle. His feet get longer and his shoulders broader every time I look at him; one day I will turn round to find that he has crossed the threshold of the mysterious cavern of adolescence, where, if I know what is good for both of us, I had better not try to follow him.[2]

The difficulty of parents and Youth making adjustment to the adolescent years can show up in the way a Youth views himself as a sexual being. Children learn to accept their sex roles within the framework of the family. Over-attachment to the mother can pose special problems by inhibiting courtship and resulting in an unwillingness on a son's part to engage in any normal relationship to the opposite sex. The family often, without realizing it, becomes the origin of sexual deviation rather than sexual normality. Unreasonable ties to the parent, rather than protecting the youth from problems of life, creates problems of adjustment.

There are other ways parents can make the period of adolescence difficult on their Youth: They may criticize excessively or attempt to repress the newly emerging values, interests, or personality of the Youth; they may be subconsciously afraid of the inactivity which will result with less responsibility for their Youth; they may be insecure in their own love relationship and despair of losing a love they can count on; they may be subconsciously jealous of the vitality, attractiveness, and intellect of their teen-ager; they may be sincerely afraid for the Youth as he breaks away to face the world; or they may be fearful that the teen-ager might do something which could cause them shame.

The Youth could accomplish emancipation much easier if parents could accept their emerging freedom without so many fears. Many parents create situations in which the teen-ager is forced either to rebel or to submit to them. Some conflict in the emancipation process is inevitable, but it can be kept to a minimum if parents and Youth realize that the gaining of independence is a desirable and necessary task for the Youth to accomplish . . . *and* the process can come about without the loss of his parent's love. Dependency and independence can coexist, one taking precedence over the other as the need demands. Parents, rather than being masters, gradually assume the role of consultant.

Lorrie McLaughlin described the conflict that arises between a mother and daughter. She says they are forever clashing about "food and clothes and makeup and curfews, and whether a new dress is really necessary, and whether the party at Nan's house is going to be chaperoned, and whether a tomato is ripe enough to use in a salad." [3]

During the early Youth years, competition and hostility between mother and daughter starts to seep to the surface. Almost
overnight, the daughter becomes an authority on everything,
especially fashions and makeup. Mothers hear: "Surely you are
not going to wear *those* shoes out in public . . . . Moth--er, you
simply can't go out with a skirt that length . . . . Mother, please
don't wear that dark lipstick. *Nobody* who is anybody ever
wears red lipstick anymore."

Sometimes they are a little more tactful and begin by, "Now
don't take this the wrong way," or "I don't want to hurt your
feelings, . . . but . . . ."

The mother may feel that Coco Chanel and Emily Post or
Amy Vanderbilt have suddenly moved into the house with her.

Miss McLaughlin speaks from the viewpoint of the mother
when she says rather fatalistically that there does not have to
be a reason you can pinpoint or identify for the conflict between
mother and daughter. It is just there and you have to learn to
live with it.

Youth's Emancipation Problems

Most parents can learn to cope with the problems of youth's
breaking away earlier and easier than the youth can do so.
Youth's frustrations may be carry-overs from built-up resentment in childhood. One young man tells about the problems with
his father. The father would never come to watch him play football. He was hurt. He even withdrew from his friends whose
fathers did come to watch them play. He withdrew from his
father. He began making lower grades. He said: "I showed this
resentment by doing the opposite of what he told me to do. He
wanted me to work, so I decided to loaf. He wanted me to join
the service, so I decided to go to college. Everything he planned
for me I did just the opposite. I hoped it would make him feel
hurt if I thought for myself and in this way I could get back at
him for hurting me." [4]

Teen-agers also have a hard time accepting restrictions they consider unnecessary or those which embarrass them before their peers.

The reasons, "Just because I said so" or "Just because I'm older than you" are very hard for the Youth to accept. The worker with Youth must exercise great care that he gives better reasons for faith or moral values than such easy answers. This kind of answer is certain to destroy respect between the adolescent and the worker.

Ben Shahn's statement, "You have not converted a man just because you have silenced him," also applies to relationships with Youth. Dr. Marvin C. Dubbe of Oregon State University says that it does not solve a thing for a parent to insist that his Youth "shut up." In his article, "What Parents Are Not Told May Hurt," workers with Youth are alerted to a serious danger:

> Don't shut the child off (or up) when he needs to talk. Learn to listen. Hear him out. Do this even when the words are bitter and when they are thrown as sharp barbs at your heart. (Later, he will be contrite.) It is an unfair situation when you say anything you wish (because you are bigger) but only allow the return of what you are willing to hear. You will not solve problems that way. You won't even know what the problems are! [5]

Parents often become defensive when their young person criticizes them. Many Youth are not trusted at home. Their judgments are questioned; the alliances are criticized; their interests are ridiculed; their accomplishments are not given proper honor; they are not aware of parental love.

The worker probably has several Youth under his leadership who have such problems relating to parents. Similar treatment to what the young person receives at home will, naturally, only serve to further alienate the Youth.

Consistency in the expectation of success is very important. The youth needs the freedom to try to succeed. He needs the freedom to risk failure without having blame heaped upon him. He needs to receive credit for the measure of success he attains without the nagging reminder of what he did not accomplish. He tends to see himself as he *thinks* his parents see him.

In the play *The Black Sheep,* the father nails his not-accept-able-to-society son to the wall on every count he could think of, all the while reminding him of how much he and his mother had sacrificed for him. After the emotional tongue-lashing, the mother says, "Jack, your father didn't mean what he just said." Jack replies, "Sure he means it. Now that I know what he expects of me, I'll make darn sure he's not disappointed!" [6]

Parental favoritism is another serious problem many Youth have to cope with. Parental favoritism decreases the adolescent's self-esteem and makes him feel hostile. What the child interprets as *favoritism* may be nothing more than his thoughtless comparison of his treatment with that given a brother or sister, but the important thing is that he feels that favoritism is being demonstrated. The simple, absent-minded error of calling one child by another child's name sets off all kinds of emotional reactions: A Youth may even feel like shouting to his dad, *Hey, look, Dad, I'm me, remember, Me.*

One girl who had had trouble establishing her own identity—accepting herself for the fine person she was—had great difficulty maturing into normal adulthood because parents and adult friends kept comparing her to her only sister who was much older than she. When she was a senior in college she was able to write to her sister about it.

Until I finished my second year in college, I lived in your shadow. There was nothing wrong with that shadow, of course, but I almost never pulled out of it. In every way, I was compared to you and what you had done and how well you had done it. Everyone was always asking me if I were going to do the same thing, meaning religious type work, etc.) ; they were constantly forgetting my name and calling me by yours. About what I was going to do, I answered, "I don't know" until I grew tired of that answer. Finally I would answer "Yes," just so they would not ask me anything anymore.

I don't know how long it takes anyone else to find themselves, or whatever *identity* is called. But, due to my withdrawal, I took longer. For awhile, I resented you; and in order to get things or to do things I wanted, I would rebel and always find some way of blaming you. As you can see, you didn't rate very high on my list.

I suppose one of the main reasons for my feeling this way was that I was so lonesome. I hated being so much younger than all of you; being the only one at home; living away from town and the kids I went to school with; my parents being so much older than everyone else's.

Well, anyway, I don't resent you any more. (Aren't you excited?) and it's a darn good thing I'm not you and you're not me. This world is in a big enough mess as it is.

It's rather funny now that I think of it. I bet mother had a heck of a time with both of us being so different. Well, since I've expounded, I'll stop and study for awhile. Write and tell me how silly I was. I really do love you.

Such a need as self-identity can be helped by a worker's show of interest.

The "Sex Barrier"

Of all the subjects difficult for Youth to discuss with their parents, sex and petting is number one. Most parents have the tendency to react with cold chills. Youth sense this attitude and feel embarrassed and uncomfortable for having brought up the subject. One teen-ager described her mother like this:

Do you know who is the great stone face? It's my mom. Especially when the subject is sex, she glazes over and just gets rigid. Honest, I wonder how she had me.[7]

Young people may even come to the erroneous conclusion that their parents disapprove of their interest in the opposite sex. Stephen Goeburg gave college students an opportunity to express honestly some of their difficult adolescent experiences. One boy talked about his escape into loneliness like this:

Because of my acne, and my parents' restrictive attitude toward girls, I was in sort of a bind. During the weekends, most of my friends were out on dates, but I was alone. I was afraid to meet girls because of my skin and my parents. At times, I would just sit in the dark and think. I wanted to be with people so much, but I was all alone. Then I would start thinking of a girl that was pretty . . . I pretended that she . . . was my girlfriend . . . But I was afraid of girls, and if I did have a girlfriend, my parents would be mad. So I had an imaginary girl.[8]

The young man was sixteen years old at the time. He ended with these poignant statements:

My parents rarely sat down and talked to me. He [his father] is very quiet. Sometimes my mother talks to me and when she does, I love her so much. Usually she just yells and lectures like most mothers. If only they could try to understand me and listen to what I say without lecturing. If I could only once leave the house without their saying a hundred times, "Watch out driving," or "Don't be late," I could love them so much more. I'd feel so much better if once they would say, "Have a good time."[9]

Psychologists and the authorities on adolescent behavior do not favor excessive parental permissiveness. In fact, the opposite seems to be true. Eric Erikson said: "The search of youth, I believe, is not for all-permissibility, but rather for new ways of directly facing up to what truly counts."[10]

Although youth protest against parental restrictions, most of them recognize their need for a certain amount of adult support and protection. Some even complain about the lack of home supervision. They want parents who can be depended on to act consistently. They need and want the security that comes from knowing exactly what they can do and what they cannot do. "They do not like to live in an uncertain world, in which the same act is punished one day and ignored the next . . . They accept strictness, if it grows out of love, better than they accept inconsistency."[11]

They need something solid to bounce against, and they need to feel that this something solid is still going to be there and still going to be solid. To be *solid* is not to be legalistically rigid and unyielding. It is not dominance without love. Youth want their parents to trust them more and worry about them less. They want to make their own decisions—with guidance. They want parents and counselors to respect their privacy. They do not want adults to crash down the gates to their inner thoughts and feelings. But believe it or not, they want adults to keep up with the world of Youth—not to try to live in that world with them, but to know what's going on; not to pass pious judgment, but to be in the know. They may want to bounce some ideas off adult values. Maybe they will even evaluate or criticize some of the things wrong with their world . . . *if* they feel adults are not trying to outmaneuver them.

Special Family Problems

It is difficult for most parents to adjust to rapid social change. Teen-agers say, "I feel so sorry for so-and-so because her parents just don't know anything that's going on in the world." Someone breaks in with, "Oh, they know, all right. They just think they can keep their precious daughter from finding out about it." Or another remark, "You know, John's mother is pitiful. She is so old-fashioned. I know he's ashamed of her."

Other parents may go to the opposite extreme. They may be such "swingers" that the Youth, subconsciously at least, thinks of them as competitors.

Some parents are so burdened with their own problems that they cannot give much attention to the problems of their children. These problems may be physical illness, financial burdens, conflict with in-laws, time-consuming jobs, or marital problems.

Many Youth live in homes broken by divorce or death, and the mother must support the family. Some live in homes where the parents are in constant discord. The parents may not know how to show love for each other nor for their children because they were deprived of affection or treated cruelly when they were children. Some live with relatives. Some live in homes where they know they are not wanted. Some have a parent in prison.

Some live in poverty. Children from financially handicapped families often have to sacrifice education to help support the family. They may be socially unacceptable to the peer group because of *where* they live or because their peers know that they are on welfare. Poverty may also make it necessary for a family to live in a delinquent area where antisocial acts are the badge of maturity. "When poverty is combined with lack of parental affection and defects of parental character, the adolescent's basic need for security and support in the family circle is not met." [12]

Everybody's gotta have a home, but not everybody is happy with the home he's got. We will talk more about the socially and economically deprived Youth in the chapter, "Where Have All the Others Gone?"

Family life should offer the basic core for mutual respect, trust, love and ethics. There are many youth in America today who are living in unfavorable home situations. Youth leaders need to be aware of the tremendous impact the home has on the Youth they seek to lead, and to realize that during adolescence there is a slackening of influence on the part of both good and bad parents. Very often, a leader or teacher in public school or church may become a great enough influence on a Youth's life to effect his entire destiny.

This opportunity is one of the awesome privileges of trying to understand Youth!

1. David Prewett, "Contemporary Youth and Family Relationships: The Alienated and Their Families," *Southern Baptist Family Life Education*, January-March, 1968, p. 3.

2. H. Knowles, editor, *Gentlemen, Scholars, and Scoundrels* (New York: Harper and Brothers, 1959), p. 230.

3. Lorrie McLaughlin, "Daughters Should Leave Home!" *Home Life*, January 1, 1969, p. 37.

4. Stephen J. Goeburgh, *The Experience of Adolescence* (Cambridge: Schenkman Publishing Co., 1965), pp. 35-36.

5. *Family Life Co-ordinator*, XIV, No. 2 (April, 1965), pp. 51-118.

6. Dorothy Russell Murphree, *The Black Sheep* (Chicago: The Dramatic Publishing Company, 1966), p. 12.

7. Charlie W. Shedd, *The Stork Is Dead* (Waco: Word Books, 1968), p. 15.

8. *Op. cit.*, Goeburgh, pp. 109-110.

9. *Ibid.*

10. Erik H. Erikson, *Youth, Identity, and Crisis* (New York: W. W. Norton, 1968), p. 37.

11. *Op. cit.*, Strang, pp. 389-390.

12. *Ibid.*, 364.

Chapter 6. WHERE DO I BELONG?

LIKE A PENDULUM, loyalties swing—away from parents who have been the number one influence in the child's life to the peer group. The group reassures the adolescent that he is not in the boat of life by himself. Most youth want to be emancipated from their parents. Some do not trust anyone over thirty. Others are finding out about and experimenting with the new drives and urges produced by their changing bodies. Most youth find safety in numbers.

Everybody needs to feel that *somebody* (preferably a lot of somebodies) likes him just because he is likeable. Everybody needs to belong to somebody—by free choice.

Frankie Addams, the twelve-year-old gangling girl in Carson McCuller's play *The Member of the Wedding,* expressed this longing for acceptance in classic words. Her mother had been dead for as long as she could remember. She thought her father didn't know she existed. Her only brother, Jarvis, was about to get married and go away forever. The day before the wedding, she said: "The trouble with me is that for a long time I have been just an "I" person ... All people belong to a "we" except me ... Not to belong to a "we" makes you too lonesome." [1]

She went on to talk about her brother and the girl he would marry the next day and said that she loved them so much because "they are the *we* of me."

Most youth choose the person or persons to make their *we* from their own or slightly higher socio-economic groups.

Adolescents, perhaps more than any other age group, want to make it on their own with their friends. The vocation of a youth's father may dictate the general social circle in which the family moves. The location of his parents' house may determine the school he attends. The family income may limit the way he dresses and the amount of money he spends on friends or dates. But in spite of all these underlying parental controls on his general social structure, he wants and needs to feel that he has the right to choose and be chosen by the group he calls his friends.

Making friends is an important task for the adolescent. He must still rely on parents for advice; yet, he more and more seeks friends who can serve as confidants. His preference is for the company of his peers. "He is instinctively right in caring most of all for how they reckon him; although his harshest critics, they are still most tolerant of his foibles." [2]

The group provides the youth with an outlet for healthy rebellion. He can continue to live at home in his family situation, but he has the support of his peers on ideas and actions that might be contrary to those of his parents.

The adolescent wants to learn how to get along with agemates of both sexes, how to make friends, and how to work with others for a common purpose. In order to accomplish these goals, they feel strong motivation to learn social skills which will enable them to relate to their peers. They overwhelmingly feel the need to be accepted by a circle of friends. Therefore, they develop whatever habits or skills will enable them to be accepted.

This concern to be liked by peers was found to be the dominant common denominator running through almost all of the compositions from the local high school survey referred to earlier. Even those who said they were happy as "loners" and those who said they did not care what others thought of them usually revealed a hidden longing to be accepted.

Boy.—I like to be admired by younger people more than older people. I would rather anything else happen to me than have a friend mad at me or think I am stuck up.

Girl.—I would like to be a good person—nice to know and well-liked.

Girl.—I am concerned with what other people think of me. I am often bitter toward people and life. I think I am sorty (sic) of shy. I can't get to know anyone easily. I hope other people think of me as good. I think most of my friends think I'm fun to be with. People think I'm friendly.

17-year-old girl.—I am a religious type person and find many of my friends, both boys and girls, have nothing in common with me. I am very self-conscious, and this is a handicap. If I don't know the crowd I'm in, I turn terribly shy. I wish I could love everyone the way I'm supposed to. (She went on to say that she wanted to become a missionary so her life would not be lived in vain.)

19-year-old boy, a senior in high school.—I have no idea what other people think of me and it really doesn't mean a whole lot to me. I am what I am and there's not much I or anybody else can do about it. (But on the kind of person he would like to become, he said: "I want to become a well-liked person to all the people I know.")

18-year-old boy, a senior in high school.—I'm the kind of person who doesn't like being with other people. It's not that I don't like people. It's just that I never have and never will fit in with the other kids. (*But,* notice his goals in life: "I plan to finish high school, attend college, and become an accountant. I then plan to marry a girl I love very much and raise a wonderful family and finally to die a happy old man.")

19-year-old girl who was a high school senior.—I think I am a well-liked person, otherwise people would not run around with me like they do ... I am a very religious person and friendly—I speak to everyone I see.

A high school girl who lived with her father, stepmother and four stepbrothers and sisters.—I think I am a very different person from a lot of people. I enjoy keeping to myself, and hate to talk out loud ... I would love to be a very religious and helpful person. I wouldn't want to be someone everybody knows, just a very helpful person who cares about other people.

Some of these youth seemed overly-confident of their age-mates' friendship. Some of them were hoping for friendship, but afraid they did not have it. Others were absolutely certain they have been left out, so they sought ways to compensate: "enjoying" aloneness, trying to love without expecting love in return, giving themselves to service vocations, becoming what some of the teens described as a "religious type" person. Are not most of these expressions a longing to find the answer to the questions: Where do I belong? To whom do I belong? For many young people, the answer is found in one special friend. Later, it is found in one special *group* of friends called *the clique.*

The Clique—Pros and Cons

The *clique* is the first transitional institution that is independent of adult supervision and control. In the early youth years, this group is composed of the same sex. Girls' cliques are much more elaborate and complicated than boys' cliques. However, boys cliques remain united through the twelfth grade because of the athletic culture, whereas girls' cliques disintegrate earlier because of individual competition in dress and dates.

The *clique* usually refers to the in-school group and the *gang* to the out-of-school group. There is a current trend to replace the word *clique* with the word *crowd.*

Call it what you will, belonging to the crowd is very important to an adolescent. Gordon says that through such group membership, dates are arranged and experimentation in liquor, sex, and smoking are provided and discussed. Styles in clothes are set and moral reputations made and broken.

Informal leadership of high and low ranks emerge in the cliques and gangs. In fact, there seems to be a definite hierarchical pattern among the leadership in each group and also *between* the crowds and gangs. Some of them are the wheels, others the brains. The athletic crowd may be called "the jocks," and the drinking crowd, the "beer boys," etc. Each member knows the status system.

Girls strive to get into the good groups. The group is most important to the girls. They talk with the girls in their group about how to attract that certain boy. They help each other. They plan what to wear, what to say, which side of the hall to walk down, which door to go through at church, how long to wait at their locker, which drive-in restaurant to circle, and how many times to circle it, etc. *ad infinitum*. Later, they check up on how well their strategy worked. They may do this checking at a slumber party or over the telephone. They repeat every word the boy said, every word she said, describe exactly how he raised his left eyebrow, how he turned his head, how he slouched, how he grinned, even what he smelled like. This routine is told over and over and over, until the date becomes less fun than the telling.

The youth who tells his parents, "Everyone's doing it," means only those who are important to him at the time—either his own friendship group or the style and pattern setters in his school. They really mean those in *the top clique* are doing it.

The group or the clique idea is by its very nature exclusive. Some cliques are in. Some are out. Some are valued as good cliques, some as bad. *Seventeen,* (September, 1968) carried an article, "The Clique Mistique: The Ins and Outs of High School Society." The writers pointed out that groups sometimes use each other as punching bags or scapegoats and then said to the girls, "Many of you apparently have a need—a childhood hangover—to look at life as 'good guys' versus 'bad guys.' "

The article quotes a girl who was trying to make the case that her crowd was democratic. She said: "One of us is rich and one lives by the railroad tracks. One is Catholic. One is Greek. One is Jewish. I'm Protestant. We hang around together all the time.

If a creepy kid wanted to get in with us, we'd be nice and friendly, but we wouldn't hang around with her. Creepy kids have their own creepy crowds." [3]

She *thought* she was democratic, but she was using her "democratic" group to express snobbism and superiority to another group.

One 11th grader justified the undemocratic part of the clique like this:

> I think the whole school is made up of cliques but some of them aren't as exclusive as others. I think cliques are the normal thing, and I don't really see anything wrong with them. After all, in your whole life there are going to be people who are 'above' and 'below' and school is no different. We live in a democracy, but we don't have lunch with the Vanderbilts . . . A person has to accept the fact that everyone has their own little group of friends." [4]

The clique serves many useful purposes. Ernest A. Smith in *American Youth Culture,* lists six:

1. It provides the first and probably most important span in the structural bridge linking childhood and adulthood.
2. It lays the foundation for association between equals.
3. It provides the first step in the essential shift of affection from the parents.
4. It helps to reinforce the acceptance of the sex role, especially for the boys.
5. Cliques give their members status, companionship, security, and acceptance.
6. They help to promote social adjustment and social skills. [5]

Sugarman and Hochstein point out these facts: The group offers reassurance and a sounding board for the teens, provides ready-made company, lends courage to the inexperienced, and brings social life into manageable proportions. "You are at least a Somebody in your own small group and, in consequence, are more likely to feel at home in the complex world of mass education." [6]

On the negative side of the ledger, these same authors point out:

1. The clique increases inability to move from one group to another. Once you're in, you're stuck.
2. The clique is exclusive. In order to grow as a human being, the youth need to know and understand as many different kinds of people as possible. The clique limits that opportunity.
3. The group has a way of diminishing identity. "In" can be an abbreviation for "indistinguishable."

Friedenberg points out as immeasureably destructive that kind of conformity "that abandons the experience of the individual in order to usurp a tradition to which he does not belong and to express a view of life foreign to his experience and, on his lips, phony." [7]

The best and the worst results from the clique can easily be seen. It can operate as a loose knit group—providing reassurance, ready companionship for a spur-of-the-minute shopping trip or movie, and comfortable, congenial "regulars" for a slumber party.

The clique can also operate at the most spiteful level. One girl's word may be law and order. The clique members may talk about her behind her back (many of them seemingly despising her), but then pay homage to her in a kind of eerie, cult-like worship.

Parents and Youth leaders cannot eradicate the group nor its influence. Whether church Youth are insiders or outsiders, they cannot escape the influence of the group. How the group affects them depends to a large extent on how they understand and relate to it.

The Crush

Adolescents often form a crush-like attachment with agemates of the same sex, or with teachers and counselors. Strang says that, "If wisely handled, This experience can meet an adolescent's real need for acceptance, for help in understanding and dealing with his upsurging impulses, and for an ideal to imitate. If unwisely handled by a person who is frightened by the relation and breaks it off suddenly or by a person who has a neurotic need for the adolescent's devotion, the experience may result in a withdrawal from any close relationship in the future, or in a permanent homosexual orientation." [8]

The teen-age girl may fall in love with a married man—her minister, her favorite teacher, a man in whose home she baby-sits. In so doing, she is testing her ability to love a man with someone she knows is safe—someone who will not expect her to follow through in responsibility. Some teen-age boys go through the same attachment to a married woman. This kind of experience can be a healthy transfer of emotions from parents to the opposite sex. Leaders of church Youth should be aware of this need for junior highs (and sometimes senior highs) to develop this attachment to respected adults of the same or opposite sex. They need not become overly alarmed when such a crush develops, but they do not need to encourage the attachment. A brusque closing of a relationship which was always an open one may frighten, embarrass, and humiliate the Youth to the point where he will drop out of the school or church activity. On the other hand, it is cruel to take advantage of an adolescent's emotions. To hold the youth's affection is to discourage relationships with their own age-mates.

Many an adult teacher and leader has served (often without realizing it) as a good and wholesome love object for a youth as the girl or boy learns to transfer emotions from father and mother to some young man or young woman. They do this by accepting the crush for what it is, and nothing more.

First Loves

In the later adolescent years, the cliques—usually composed of members of one sex—are replaced by the crowd which includes boys and girls. At first, crowds have little dating between members, but they do provide an opportunity for meeting approved persons of the opposite sex. It is usually in this mixed group that interpersonal experiences are built up toward increasing intimacy until the person is ready to date. The first date—of the boy-asks-girl kind—is often to a crowd activity.

According to one survey of the girls, fourteen- to sixteen-year-old, 70 percent reported dating. Ninety percent over age sixteen said they dated regularly.

Early dating (ages twelve and thirteen) may cause many problems. This age youth usually is not socially mature enough to carry on a conversation, nor to feel at ease and make the other person feel at ease. Of course, some teen-agers are ready for dates sooner than others. The date will be discussed in more detail in chapter 8. What many junior high's call "going to-gether" does not involve a date as such. It means that the boy walks the girl to and from classes, or to the bus after school. It means that he sits with her at the ball games and is "with her" at group parties.

Adults should not look lightly on the teen-ager's first love—his being in love with love. Youth's longing to love and to be loved are the emotional materials which make for religious insight and deep spiritual experience.

Puppy love can be serious. Strang reports knowing a fourteen-year-old boy and girl who committed suicide when their parents tried to keep them apart. Workers with Youth should recognize and sympathize with young people's ardent feelings.

There are positive values in the early love affairs. The youth is learning to be unselfish, to love and care for another person, to handle normal and desirable emotions, and to accept another person as he is. He learns what it means to be loyal to someone.

Out of His Head

Adults need to realize that teen-age love is more intense and absorbing than mature love. With a little exercise of the memory, the worker will recall the terrible intensity of that think-of-nothing-else kind of love. Smith says that the romantic love complex is characteristic of modern America and may be described as "a kind of emotional seizure, based on overwhelming sex attraction. The lover is incapable of thinking of anything but the love-object." [9] This romanticism is a carry over from the old idea that two people were destined for each other from the beginning and brought together by fate for eternity. They were supposed to recognize each other in an instant experience called "love at first sight." For many years, this romantic love complex has been nurtured by movies, songs, and sweet stories. Traditionally, courtship and marriage in America has been founded on the romantic love idea. But there are disadvantages to this approach. Overemphasis on romantic love makes the lover subject to irrational acts. He becomes subject to illusion, delusions, compulsions, and even symptoms of mental abnormality, so that he lives in a world of his own with his own private standards. He literally "goes out of his head" over the loved object. The couple becomes "mad" about each other.

Such an unrealistic idealization of the loved one attaches qualities to the person which he does not possess. It usually leads to extreme jealousy where the person thinks he owns the love-object like a piece of property which is his to protect. This attitude is poor preparation for marriage. The glamour of romantic love may make adjustment to the routine of married life difficult. Intense can't-live-without-you romantic love often leads to hasty and ill-prepared-for marriages which try to ignore all differences in religious and cultural backgrounds.

As the romantic love complex comes in and takes over two by two, the couples tend to separate from the crowd. The crowd gradually disintegrates. In some teen cultures in America today, there is a tendency to skip the crowd phase and go directly from the clique stage to the date and romantic love stage.

Refer to Appendix A for a more detailed discussion of sex and dating.

1. Carson McCullers, "The Member of the Wedding," *American Dramatic Literature*, Jordon Y. Miller, editor (New York: McGraw-Hill Book Co., 1961), p. 443.

2. Gene Usdin, M.D., editor, *Adolescence: Care and Counseling* (Philadelphia: J. B. Lippincott Co., 1967), p. 11.

3. Daniel A. Sugarman and Rollie Hochstein, "The Clique Mistique: The Ins and Outs of High School Society," *Seventeen*, September, 1968, p. 137.

4. C. W. Gordon, *The Social System of the High School* (Glencoe, Illinois: Glencoe Free Press, 1957), p. 109.

5. Ernest A. Smith, *American Youth Culture* (Glencoe, Illinois: Glencoe Free Press, 1962), p. 72.

6. Sugarman and Hochstein, *The Social System of the High School* (Glencoe, Illinois: Glencoe Free Press, 1957), p. 137.

7. E. Z. Friedenberg, *Coming of Age in America* (New York: Random House, 1965), p. 13.

8. *Op. cit.*, Strang, p. 326.

9. Ronald Goldman, *Readiness for Religion* (New York: Seabury Press, 1965), p. 117.

Chapter 7. THE YOUTH CURTAIN

TODAY'S TEENS live in overlapping ages: the atomic age, the jet age, the space age, the age of automation, and an age that soon may be labeled the age of protest.

They live in a society bewildered by the accelerated rate of change. The life of Western man has changed more in the past three generations than it did in the preceding 2,000 years. Technology is changing so rapidly that a job of today may vanish within a generation or even a decade. Generations change—not every twenty-five years, but every *five* years.

The adolescent, then, is literally swept on the tidal wave of change. Time does not pause for a new tradition to form. Eric Erickson, the Harvard professor who has spent over twenty years measuring and testing human behavior said, "In such a time all thinking about man becomes an experiment in living," because man will not hold still long enough to be studied or measured.

Change is not limited to technology. Technological changes produce new problems in the areas of ethics and morals. "The gigantic bomb and the tiny pill, which, if they do not give man power over life and death, certainly give him the decision as to whose life and whose death it shall be." [1]

There is also rapid social change. Youth lives in an unstable world. It is in constant flux. It is more than ever before an age of social mobility. The youth is not rigidly tied to the class of his birth. Cultural patterns are also constantly changing. Rowena Ferguson asserts that within one generation the United States has shifted its cultural pattern. Previously, ethnic and racial minority groups related to a dominant white, Anglo-Saxon, Protestant majority. Suddenly, American society finds itself developed into cultural, racial, and religious pluralism.

The youth is expected to relate to a society which is full of paradoxes:

Communication satellites instantly relay television programs (and commercials of things to eat, wear, use, operate, and play with) to every part of the world—but humanity agonizes over its inability to communicate.

Space exploration speeds to new discoveries at a speed that staggers the imagination—but man has not learned how adequately to control his movements and the use of space within his atmosphere.

Americans have diligently pursued freedom—yet are now asking *freedom for what?*

The United States is a nation of power. She has sufficient nuclear warheads to *kill* all the people on the earth several times over—yet power has not solved the frustrations of the people who live on the earth.

Our nation is one of wealth, made up of people of knowledge. In two seconds, machines now do mathematical problems that would take a man thirty-eight years to solve. Copy machines, computers, sophisticated equipment of every description abounds—yet fewer and fewer individuals feel capable of understanding their world.

Paradox upon paradox faces youth.

The adolescent must relate to parents and adults who still

think and dream of a quasi-rural background, but the adolescent of the 70's lives in an urban society. By 1968, 73% of Americans lived on 1% of the land. Even those youth who still live in rural areas or small towns are urban in attitude and thought patterns because of the mass media: television, transistors, magazines, and newspapers. There is no hiding place from this age of secularization, and indeed few youth are looking for a hiding place in a society which allows few secrets.

Each youth must discover—in this society—who he is and where he is going. He is frightened and disturbed that he may become what his elders seem to be. He does not fully trust the adult. He holds deep within his being the belief that he can do a better job of it all. So he consolidates his efforts with the other youth around him and they form a tightly knit society of their own. Sociologists have tagged this society with names like subculture, sub-society, or youth culture.

Why the Youth Curtain?

The solid front and attempts to conceal their behavior are universal characteristics of youth. They want to hide their activities so they can relate to their environment on their own terms, free from the supervision of adults.

Actually, the peculiar development of a Youth subculture is a recent development which has come about in stages over the past twenty-five years. The term "teen-ager" did not appear in the dictionary until about thirty years ago, and the distinctive aura we throw around the teen-age phenomenon appeared even later than that.

James Coleman made a study of 8,000 American youth and found that the youth culture is definitely becoming stronger in modern middle class suburbia. In the lower income groups, the youth must go to work very early in order to help support the family. He is not so caught up in the separate youth culture.

In reality, this youth culture is not a separate, independent culture. Its behavior patterns are most often modifications of the adult structure.

Why this withdrawal? this seclusion? this banning together? The primary function of the youth subculture is that of bringing about the normal movement from the parental family into which he was born to the establishment of his own family. To accomplish this task, an adolescent must loosen dominant bonds of affection from his parents in order to strengthen heterosexual bonds.

Some mothers literally cut off the strings of an apron and present them as a wrapped engagement present to their son's fiancee. But actually, aided by the security afforded him through the youth subculture, the youth has cut (perhaps "torn off" would be a better expression) those apron strings many years earlier. The subculture helps him to fly. He is sustained by the thousands of other youth who are also breaking the filial ties. He is no longer willing to wait stoically for *someday*. He is asking, *Why not me? Why not now?*

This withdrawal from adult association and adult confidence produces what seems to the adult to be a rebellion against the adult society and its established ethics. It is the rare adolescent, however, who totally rejects the adult world. He handles it, tries it on for size, alters it to fit his person and personality, adds a dash of color here and a new fad there, and comes up with a personalized modification of the adult world.

The conflict of generations begins at that point in maturing when children turn away from parents to peer groups. "When adults observe that a large proportion of youth is becoming threateningly unfamiliar and uncongenial there is said to be a youth problem, and deliberate efforts are made to induce or compel the youth to accept and participate in the dominant culture." [2]

The adults who become overly concerned with what they call a youth problem may condemn the youth culture. However, if the adult institution *attacks* the youth culture, it has the effect of unifying teen-agers to the further rejection of adult influence.

Youth Culture Language

Youth develop their own language which becomes a way—sometimes friendly, sometimes hostile—to eliminate the danger of adult eavesdropping. This secrecy of expression closes communications with adults and provides a safeguard against dominant adult-forced ethics. Not only does the subculture of youth exclude outsiders, it sets the members apart in their own world. When adults get in on the know, the language changes.

Adults should not try to break the language barrier while working on the communication gap. A medical doctor who specializes in the care of adolescents says: "I find it necessary to understand the current mores and language of the adolescent, but equally important to speak to them in my own language, to maintain my own mores and not to attempt to be one of them." [3]

Language is one area of the youth culture which seems to be handed down from those who are just emerging from it. One analyst asserts that the college campuses are the slang pacesetters—that slang starts and spreads on the college campuses, and finishes out its life-cycle in youth culture.

Another aspect closely akin to the language barrier is the intentional subtle deception of adults. This deception is quite often accomplished by feeding an adult enough "youth secrets" to permit him to believe that he is in on the youth know, while actually the real secrets of the group are well protected.

One teen-age boy said, after he returned from a choir retreat: "The minister of music stayed up with our room of boys all night. He thought he could be a Good Joe with us and we'd break down and tell him everything. But we didn't tell him anything important—just enough to make him think he was 'in.'"

A teen-age girl expressed her feelings to *Dear Abby:*

> I've never written to you before, but the girl who signed herself "No Privacy" really got to me because I had the same kind of mother.

I finally solved my problem by keeping *two* diaries. One
for myself, and one for my mother to read. I sort of "hid"
the diary I wanted my mother to read in an obvious place,
and I would even write something rather shocking in it so
she would think it was the only one I was keeping.
My real diary I hid where she wouldn't find it in a million
years. It worked like a charm. Mother was happy thinking
she knew all about me. And I was happy knowing she
didn't.[4]

This subtle deception which leaks information to the right
people at the right times serves to keep the adults off their backs
and, as the young girl said, it keeps the adults happy if they
think they know all about the adolescent.

This deception applies to youth's relationship with ministers.
Smith maintains that clergymen "isolate themselves from
groups by overemphasizing religious-moral issues and by standing as judges of behavior. In turn, youth hide their norms and
behavior behind a facade of strict conformity."[5]

Much of the secrecy connected with the youth culture appears
to protect youth from the judgment of all adults, including ministers and other professional workers with youth, especially in
the areas where sex behavior violates adult norms.

Youth Culture Norms vs. Adult Norms

Parents and leaders need to discover valid grounds for their
classifying activities as right or wrong. A thing is wrong because it is inherently hurtful to someone, not just because it is
new or not traditional. Young people feel keenly about illogical
reasoning which tags an activity as wrong without giving valid
reasons for doing so. They observe that many activities approved by the adult world are more dangerous and harmful than
some activities banned by adults. Marijuana, for example, is
not as dangerous as whiskey.

Probably the most important area where adults try to enforce
their norms on youth is in the area of sex. The youth culture ap-
proves customs of sexual expression that are tabooed by adults.
Petting is a widespread and accepted activity in dating and

courtship of youth. The youth looks on it as an acceptable form of sexual (in a healthy sense) release (See Appendix A). The adult's forced dominance in this area may be due to fear or to an awareness of the emotional forces which they know youth to be unable to control. Nonetheless, a very profound difference in behavior is found between youth and adult ideals.

One young man expressed the conflict of the adult and youth sex norms like this:

> Society is like a parent, never willing to recognize the child's capability of independence. It is like a whole group of mothers and fathers acting as one, much like my own, sitting at the dining room table passing judgment on something I have asked permission to do. . . . The desire to engage in sexual activity, drinking, and even profanity exists within me, but so does a stronger conscience which says "no." It's a constant struggle between mother on one shoulder and a desire to conform with the peer group on the other . . .[6]

The clique sets norms that are more authoritarian than those set by parents and other adults. Since there are many cliques even within one school, there would be many norms. The clique acts as a protective structure for its members.

One of the basic needs of members of the youth culture is to be accepted and identified with certain peer groups. This acceptance usually requires rigid conformity to certain patterns of behavior. Clique conformity is far-reaching. It includes dress, language patterns, selection of friends, and even who and who not to date. It controls attitudes toward adult persons and institutions, especially the police, parents, teachers, and the church. Of course, there is no physical coercion put on the clique members to conform, but they are motivated to toe the line by ridicule and isolation of the nonconformers and praise and admiration for the conformers.

Approval of the clique is most important. One girl said: "If you're an insider, everything you do is right. If you're an outsider, no matter what you do, it's wrong." [7] Smith says that to be rejected by the in group may result in withdrawal and isolation for many individuals. Some find escape in fantasy or daydreaming. Many drop out of school or possibly leave home. Fear of ridicule becomes a constant pressure toward conformity.

In certain groups, even on the high school level, drug experimentation is "in" and a youth is "out" if he doesn't go along. A medical doctor and psychiatrist, Dr. John L. Schimel, said: "In certain groups if you haven't tried pot, if you haven't been on a Benzedrine party, you are 'out'. . . . The use of drugs is part of the social scene. . . . I see youngsters whose complaint is that they don't have the guts to try marijuana and they feel awfully bad about this." [8]

It is extremely difficult for an adult to comprehend the pressure the teen-ager feels between the youth culture norms and adult norms. A high school junior was trying to describe a girl to her mother. She said: "She's not a class officer, nor a cheer leader, nor a straight *A* student, nor a member of a good group; so she just blends into nothingness."

The Glamour Trap and the Sex Swindle

From junior high on for the girls, it's underclothes to identify with womanhood; charm schools offered by the leading department stores; shampoo, rinses, highlights, setting lotion, and shines for the hair, as well as electric hair setters and dryers; can after can of hair spray; five or six items for the care and beauty of the nails; deodorants (spray, cream, pat-on, roll-on, powder-on); soaps, facials, and dozens of skin care products; "gook" guaranteed to hide blemishes and "erase" eye wrinkles on fifteen-year-olds; base make-up; tons of eye make-up with just right eyelash curler or false eyelashes; lipstick (frosted, plain, and super-creamed) or lip gloss which promises moist, dewy, sexy lips; and . . . finally powder, either plain, pressed, transluscent, or medicated. No, powder is not *finally*. The "smell good" items are finally—the just right fragrance in bath oil, body powder, cologne, and perfume. These "scents" are available by such enticing names as *My Sin, Tabu, Intimate, One*

Night of Love, Always Mine, and *Midnight.*

A girl's status may depend on choosing the right brand name of any one of these items from the many competitors on the market.

Teen-age boys' cosmetics and toilet articles are produced by an ever-increasing business, too: deodorants, lotions, colognes, hair grooming and shaving supplies. Deodorants are available in roll-on, spray, powder, and stick forms. There are all-purpose and after-shave lotions and colognes in numerous aromas which are given exotic and intriguing names with Oriental, Asian, English, Continental, and American connotations. Scented soaps are now included in men's departments.

One of the first observations of a small-city barber was that teen-age boys unhesitatingly pay $3.00-$6.00 for a razor cut, while only a year before they complained about spending $1.50 for a regular haircut. He stated further that boys are mainly concerned with full hair and neatness. They are much more conscious of the neatness of their hair than in past years. Bleaching and coloring are almost non-existent for teen-age boys. Current hair styles are pictured by a professional magazine for barbers as containing such characteristics as strong, forward movement, sculptured design, sophisticated lines, professional look, easy to maintain, neat but not strict, and with a natural effect.

Advertisers play on the adolescent's need to be accepted by the group. The teen-age market is a big one and cosmetics comprise a large segment of the marketable items.

Thus, it is almost impossible to escape the glamour trap. Girls grow up having to cope with the forcefully promoted concept that in order to participate in romantic love, they have to have the features of Miss America: sex appeal, natural good looks, a well-proportioned body, good clothes, a broad smile with sparkling teeth. Girls respond to these romantic demands by buying tons of cosmetics and spending hours applying them.

Glamour does serve a function for American women. Since they are largely excluded from economic and political power, they use glamour to attain superiority—so much so that feminine appeal is used as a manipulative device in business, politics, and social spheres.

These glamour trappings can be deceptive. They put so much emphasis on the packaging of a person and so little on the content. Many girls wear clothes designed to emphasize sex appeal, but their personalities remain very cold and closed. Maybe there is more truth than humor in the saying, "She finally trapped a man," when a girl uses glamour trappings to cover up for less than attractive attitudes and values.

The Dollar Mark

The adolescent influences both the economy and political situation of adult society. In 1965, there were some 24 million people—or one eighth of the population of the United States—between the ages of thirteen and nineteen. By 1975, approximately 64 million persons in the United States will be under fifteen years of age, while close to another 50 million will be between the ages of fifteen and twenty-five. They spend over twelve billion dollars a year. The teen market is of especially great importance to the clothing, record, cosmetic, and sportsgood manufacturers.

Business and industry are interested in seeing that the adolescent's tastes become fads. They can often sell him specialized junk that most adults would reject.

Today's teen-agers have grown up in a period of economic security and rapid economic development. Though there are many disadvantaged youth, the middle- and upper-class youth know nothing of the depression or recession years their parents may have experienced.

What adults consider a luxury, young people consider a necessity. Records and cosmetics are two examples. One has only to look at magazines aimed toward the teen market to become aware of the tremendous advertising bombardments teens face.

A careful study of one major magazine aimed at the teenage market revealed that of its 228 pages, there was the equivalent of 168 full pages of advertising and 12 more full pages picturing popular singing groups whose clothing was advertised as available at certain stores for a specified number of dollars.

The primary financial status symbol for the boy is the automobile. It is more than a means of transportation. "It is the nearest replacement our society has for a puberty rite for our young males, and the boy has finally arrived as a full-fledged member of his subculture when he no longer is dependent on reluctant parents to taxi him about." [9]

Teen-age boys have not escaped the dollar sign in the eyes of the Madison Avenue executives. Many of them are influenced by young adult magazines which appeal not only to the craze for cars and fashion tastes of the young men, but often emphasize the life-is-for-pleasure-only philosophy. Spend freely. Spend selfishly. Take what you want . . . now. Enjoy sex without responsibility. Then spend more money . . . on yourself and if you are in an especially generous mood, spend some on your playmate—your *temporary* playmate, that is. The bulk of the teen-age market, however, is comprised of youth who have normal, healthy tastes and enough money to satisfy more of his yearnings than any previous generation of recent history.

Where does the adolescent get all of his money? Financial dependence on adults is a major fly in the ointment of youth integrity. Because of labor laws, most youth depend on parents to finance their desires.

Since modern society requires a longer and longer period of economic dependence (because of longer periods of vocational training), youth's activities fall under a longer period of parental control.

Many teen-agers, of course, have part-time jobs. Others have responsible summer jobs, but few are able to be financially independent of their parents.

The Communication Gap

James F. Adams, in *Understanding Adolescence*, says that the adult world derives its confusion from a fear that the chaotic world will become more chaotic in the future as a result of the next generation falling apart. This fear may come in part from a stereotyped image adults have of youth. The very fact that a subculture has emerged tends to make adults edgy, uneasy. The attempt to understand youth (even the study of such a book as this) without accepting them as persons may produce a wrong image in the adult's mind. A communication gap will surely result if an adult learns general characteristics of the contemporary youth subculture and ignores the individual differences or the age differences of youth within the culture.

While there has always been a communication gap between adults and youth, the two worlds are further apart today than they have ever been in the past. The gap is not necessarily bad, and does not necessarily indicate distrust. Rather, the differences occur because of the different influences each generation has had during its growing-up years. Since progress has been so great in recent years, the influences brought about by progress have caused tremendous differences in viewpoints. The added familiarity youth have with peoples of the world—due to instant communication media—has given rise to a virtually spontaneous feeling among youth over much of the world that men must learn to live together in peace.

These differences are felt in personal ways, too. The influence of mobility, of observing what others are doing, of listening incessantly to a transistor radio, of constant bombardment of values which are opposed to those taught the youth, the more intensive education, and many others all combine to force the youth to fashion his life out of a wider range of choices than he has ever had before.

Eric Erickson, the psychoanalyst, predicts that the future will see a tragic reevaluation on the part of those youth who have attempted to ritualize life for themselves against adults. He also predicts that, in the face of such provocation and challenge, adults will realize that they have abdicated too willingly and too quickly their vital roles as critics. "For without some leadership—and, if need be, leadership that can be lustily resisted—the young humanists are in danger of becoming irrelevant and ending up, each individual and each clique, stewing in strictly episodical 'consciousness expansion.' " [10]

Granted that the generation gap exists and perhaps should exist, should adults throw up their hands and make no effort to communicate? What keeps coming through as the crucial message *from the adolescent* is the necessity to maintain communication channels.

Reuel L. Howe said, "The purpose of communication, and therefore of education, is not to give people answers but to help them work out their own relation to a truth." [11] In other words, why is communication with youth necessary? To give them all the answers to the questions of life? No, for communications is not mere *telling*. It is impossible to communicate without *listening*. Perhaps the most important message an adult can receive from his study of youth is: *listen to them*. Church Youth know that adults have insights gained from experience, but church Youth also are convinced that their generation has insights into the Christian message which have been missed by adults. They want adults to hear their viewpoints. They feel that questions which are valid to faith and vital to life are being ignored and swept under the rug. They cannot understand such refusal to face up to important questions. Free expression allowed by adults who are willing to listen will allow Youth to grow into Christians competent to meet the challenges of a changing world. Listening is potentially one of the adult world's most vital contributions to youth. Browning says that "an atmosphere of acceptance and mutual support allows persons to *reveal* who they are, what their strengths and weaknesses are, and to face up to the areas in which they need to grow." [12]

A part of accepting a person for what he is implies accepting and living with differences. The teen-ager is not like an adult. He is not even like the adult was at the same age. No two generations are alike. When an adult says, "But I faced the same decisions when I was a young person," he not only turns a teen-ager away, he also reveals that he has not fairly evaluated the influences of a rapidly changing world on youth.

Adults who hold on to the stereotyped image that youth is bad increase the chasm between the two groups. Merton Strommen says, "This image exaggerates their distress over family and dating problems and minimizes their concern over faith and unresolved guilt. It emphasizes their involvement in questionable activities and de-emphasizes their sense of Christian vocation. Youth sense this caricature and feel unjustly judged. All of which reinforce their conviction that they are second-class citizens." [13]

Of course, youth also can erect a barrier to communication when they think of all adults as one huge over-bearing policeman. Adults are individuals, too. They have strengths and weaknesses. Browning says that to be in communication means to be an environment where both adults and youth can indirectly share any strengths they have and then become channels of God's grace and love for each other. This communication can be greatly aided by the adult's willingness to listen.

Perhaps the rawest wound on the adult's side of the communication chasm is the open disrespect on the part of the teenager. And fourteen- and fifteen-year-olds *do* often challenge their parents (especially) with open disrespect. Many parents feel that their teens do not even like them anymore. They not only are disrespectful, they are discourteous and full of biting sarcasm and criticism. This spitefulness can be interpreted as the clumsy, crude, and often uncomfortable efforts the teen-ager must make to grow up and stand on his own feet rather than continue to lean on his family. There is a kind of necessary disrespect by which a young person establishes his own autonomy. The youth's apparent alienation may simply be nothing more than emancipation acrobatics. Most of them usually hate themselves for their outbursts afterward, but they might rather die than let adults know they are ashamed.

Although it is possible for youth to get completely out of communication with adults, most of them move back and forth between the adult and youth world and make the best of both. The aim of all youth-adult efforts to communicate should be to put ideas and thoughts into a language which says the same thing to both the sender and the receiver.

Adult Reaction to the Youth Culture

There is no denying the existence of the youth subculture. What, then, is the response of adults to this subculture? Why talk about the adults' reaction to the youth culture in a book on understanding youth? Precisely because the adult's reaction, in turn, affects the youth.

Dr. Duvall suggests that one reason adults get so worked up about their teen-ager and his problems is because he forces them to face some issues they thought they had resolved during their own adolescence. "The mistakes of their own teen-agers are a two-edged sword cutting through the confidence parents thought they had established in themselves and their children." [14]

Church workers are frequently deeply troubled by youth's questions because they had questions (often the same ones) when they were young persons and refused to face them or were forced to squelch them. Unresolved, the questions and doubts haunt the subconscious. Erikson said that one generation revives the repressions of the generation before it. Youth won't let these questions stay pushed back. They want to deal with them, and they want adults to help.

The youth reminds the adult of those years when he, too, dreamed dreams; when he, too, protested against the status quo; when he, too, planned to fight injustice; when he, too, was willing to pay any price for human betterment. But the verve and fire of this past youth has been dissipated on less worthy ambitions. Caught in the financial trap and social whirlwind, the fight for survival during the depression, or the fury of war, he sees no way to turn back to his lofty ideals of youth.

Not all adults even subconsciously resent the teen-ager's dreams, either because of his own incomplete accomplishments or unfinished childhood. Most adults have genuine concern for youth and act, even when they act wrongly, out of a sense of love. A few react in the opposite extreme: they push the youth to do what they wanted to do and didn't.

Erickson claims that adolescents look for men and ideas to have faith in. As he looked back on more than twenty years of writing, research, and work as a psychoanalyst, he said, "As to youth and the question of what is in the center of its most passionate and most erratic striving, I have concluded that *fidelity* is the vital strength which it needs to have an opportunity to develop, to employ, to evoke—and to die for." [15]

If Erickson is right—about youth looking for men and women and ideas to have faith in—why are many of them still looking? He goes on to say that they fear a foolish, all-too-trusting commitment, and will express their need for faith in loud and cynical mistrust rather than get fooled. Youth will act shamelessly in the eyes of his elders out of free choice rather than be forced into something that he or his peers would consider shameful.

Youth live in a global society. They live "on the great highways of the world where the global winds blow." [16]

Youth progress toward adulthood in the midst of unrest and change. Man never strides toward any progress without unrest and change. The youth subculture provides a kind of cushion and insulation for him. He does not have to stand by himself while he tries to discover who he is and where he is going.

There are, however, two definite dangers inherent in the youth subculture. It can generate hostility toward adult society for unfair reasons, and it often supports mass values and behavior norms. It does not encourage individual self-direction. Ferguson says: "It (the youth sub-culture) may rub down the corners of individuality and turn a promising senior high into a carbon copy of some false image . . . The chief count against teen culture is that it exercises so much *irresponsible* power over the individual." [17]

Each individual must be able to uniquely express his own view of reality without *meaningless* conformity. Dr. Friedenberg says that in order for people to make sense of themselves and the world they live in, most of their behavior must be expressed in the patterns and roles available in their culture. Youth's conflict comes from having to live in *two* worlds and express himself in the patterns of a youth subculture existing within a larger general culture.

Maybe most teen-agers are not even asking adults to understand them since they do not understand themselves, but rather to love them—love them for what they are as well as for what they can become.

1. Eric H. Erikson, *Identity, Youth and Crisis* (New York: W. W. Norton, 1968), p. 41.

2. E. Z. Friedenberg, *Coming of Age in America* (New York: Random House, 1965), p. 9.

3. Gene Usdin, M.D., editor, *Adolescence: Care and Counseling* (Philadelphia: J. B. Lippincott Co., 1967), p. 144.

4. Abigail Van Buren, "Dear Abby," *Maryville-Alcoa Times*, January 20, 1969.

5. Ernest A. Smith, *American Youth Culture* (Glencoe, Illinois: The Glencoe Free Press, 1962), p. 37.

6. Stephen J. Goeburgh, *The Experience of Adolescence* (Cambridge: Schenkman Publishing Co., 1965), pp. 40-41.

7. Daniel A. Sugarman and Rollie Hoohstein, "The Clique Mistique," *Seventeen*, September, 1968, p. 241.

8. *Op. cit.*, Usdin, p. 210.

9. *Ibid.*, p. 25.

10. *Op. cit.*, Erickson, p. 37.

11. Marvin J. Taylor, editor, "The Dialogical Foundation for Christian Education," *An Introduction to Christian Education* (Nashville: Abingdon Press, 1966), p. 90.

12. Robert L. Browning, *Communicating With Junior Highs* (Nashville: Methodist Graded Press, 1968), p. 51.

13. Merton Strommen, *Profiles of Church Youth* (St. Louis: Concordia Publishing House, 1963), pp. 239-240.

14. Evelyn M. Duvall, *Today's Teen-agers* (New York: Association Press, 1966), p. 211.

15. *Op. cit.*, Erickson, p. 233.

16. Rowena Ferguson, *The Church's Ministry to Senior Highs* (Nashville: Methodist Graded Press, 1968), p. 27.

17. *Ibid.*, p. 31.

Chapter 8. CHEMISTRY, CHAUCER, AND CHEERLEADERS

IT IS FRIDAY NIGHT over at the high school. Floodlights blaze over the football field; cars swarm to the parking area; brightly clad teen-agers mill over the stands; a gaudily dressed band marches; cheerleaders cavort and scream in frenzy; and, finally, the heroes of the hour appear: the school team.

This arena is *life* to Youth. It is, to most of them, the climactic hour of the most vivid hours of life: school hours.

Those Youth come to church, an extension of the adult world, from *their* world: the high school. Often workers fail because they forget, or minimize, or misunderstand the major life activity of youth: being students. This period of life may be called "studenthood."

Pursuit of knowledge—whether chemistry or Chaucer—is not the sole aspect of studenthood. The term refers, rather, to a time of life when, by attending school, the youth is developing and becoming. While it is time of getting ready for life, *it is life*. Attending school, learning, and interacting with peers is the business of youth in the same way that earning a living, making a home, being a father, or being a mother is the life of adulthood.

The period of studenthood is actually nonrepeatable. Taking courses or returning to school later on may have value; but just as each developmental task must take place at the right time and in sequence, so studenthood must have its right time and full emphasis.

In studenthood, each youth must successfully relate the child he formerly was to the adult he is becoming. The period is far more than an interval to be lived through. It is a time of unique joy, a time of peak excitement, a time of formal and informal learning, and a time when important friendships are made between peers and with teachers.

The Social Whirl

Much of what was said in "The Youth Curtain," "Where Do I Belong?" and "The Dating Game" relates to the social whirl in the junior and senior high schools. The school sets the pattern and becomes the center for most of the social life in the community, so far as youth are concerned.

> The school is the *place* where the action is . . .
>> the stadium where the signals are called
>> the stage where the spotlight hits
>> the gymnasium where the game is played
>> the pit where the music pounds and screams
>> the floor where feet respond to the rhythmic
>>> contortions of face, torso, and limbs
>> the halls where notes are passed
>>> and people are passed . . . by
>>> and cheerleaders cut each other and cheer their
>>>> uniforms
>>> and teachers are condemned
>>> and gossip is bought and sold—
>>>> like who's smoking the weed
>>>> and who dated whom
>>> and reputation becomes a commodity
>>> and the latest edition of "who's in" is circulated
>>> and the girls who "succeed" are walked to classes
>>> and the word is passed on who has the booze

and ball players sport their new blazers.
School is the place where the action is . . .
the lockers where dates are made . . . and broken
and notebooks are loaned and borrowed
and money and homework are stolen
and lockers are "stacked"
and loners are left . . . alone.

Studenthood means to students themselves that they live in a world of their own generation. Studenthood means living in a community of youth. Though there are wide individual differences, still opportunity is open for all. In competition and in experience with other youth, students are finding out what they can achieve.

In the world of youth, students can choose friends. Many of the excluding factors of adulthood have not taken over. Social skills are developing; never again will there be such a chance to learn to interact effectively with others.

A primary task of studenthood is the learning of values. Along with social skills, character and value systems are being hammered out. Homes and schools and churches may be making glib statements about honesty and virtue; but in the real world of the school, value systems are put to the test. The tests are hard, for high school students are dependent upon peers for support, fellowship, and status. To be ridiculed is the next-to-worst fate; to be ostracized is the worst.

Against such a background, a teen-ager must decide whether he will "rat" on a friend whom he sees cheating; whether he will help another cheat by giving him work to copy; or (a more subtle problem) whether he will risk ridicule by acting at his own highest level—excelling.

These are only samples of the difficult problems. If the problems are solved, if the character skirmishes are won on the school battlefield, the student has built a character foundation for the rest of life. If he fails, he will be less well equipped to meet the severe tests of adulthood, when decisions are rarely clearcut; when the Christian ethic is challenged daily.

The Pressure for Grades

Obviously, studenthood is a time of learning, of gaining information. Now there is more to learn than ever before. The worlds of business, science, and industry make more demands for education. There is far too much pressure for college preparation and for achieving a level that will secure entrance to a "prestige" college or university.

A graduate student in a university, who had attained a very high grade average through high school and college, reflected on the meaning grades had come to have for him. He reflected on his high school days, and recalled that—unknowingly—his desire for good grades (caused by pressures by teachers, parents, and society in general) had resulted in his becoming part of an elite honor roll clique. He had unwittingly built his life around grades to the point that he had not learned to relate to the average high school peer. Consequently, though he had discovered the joy of learning, the pressure of grades had caused him to withdraw from the experience of learning about other persons.

In a locally-conducted survey, several high school youth expressed their concerns about grades:

- West Point is my biggest worry. I spend most of my spare time thinking about it. Two of my other worries are connected with the first. Both physical and mental training are important at the academy. If I keep my grades up Mr. —— [high school principal who would have to recommend him] won't lose confidence in me. I want to be popular, also, and I worry about being misunderstood by others.
- I've been worrying about school problems as long as I can remember.
- I worry about not making a passing grade in school. It rather seems foolish that I worry because all I have to do is get down and study, but it doesn't come that easy for me. Second, I worry about giving an oral report. It scares me to think about it and I worry about doing good on it.
- At the present time, the only worry I have is passing the semester tests . . . Being required to contain all the information you

have had in the first semester in four subjects worries me quite a bit.

- I know I must have a good education for the career I have chosen. Therefore, the grades I receive in school are very important to me. Because my problems can influence my future, I feel that my concern for them is just and necessary.

- The most prominent worries I have this week are the semester tests coming up. As these enemies creep closer and closer upon us, anyone who wishes to do well must feel slight pains in the neck at the thought of them. Although you may have studied hard throughout the semester, when it comes time to sift through the items of knowledge you have acquired, some things seem to have been lost in the shuffle. Or, perhaps, you never knew them at all. This is why I worry about semester tests. There just doesn't seem to be enough time for all the cramming you feel you need to do.

Grades! Grades! Grades! These ninth graders are all expressing concern over literally making the grade.

Adults may think these teens are exaggerating their concern, but one of their biggest worries is grades. And rightly so, because of the society in which they must cope.

Friedenberg [1] says that the school endorses and supports the patterns of behavior of certain segments of the population, while it instills in others a sense of inferiority and a warning that the rest of society considers them to be troublesome and untrustworthy. In other words, if you don't make it in the public school system (academically at least) you've had it. The grading system is the Great Divide. This Great Divide alters individuals: their values and sense of personal worth. *If I can't make the grade, I must be a nobody.*

One nineteen year old boy, a senior in high school, expressed it like this: "I would like to make good grades in all my school subjects. But I am having trouble. I think over all I am just about a failure ... Other people I guess think I am just average. Because no one knows what kind of grades I make ... I would like to be a person with high scholastic averages."

Strang verifies the fact that most students are concerned about passing and that they experience anxiety over not being able to do well. "Some students have failed so often that they are afraid to try again; their tenseness and anxiety interfere with learning." [2] She says that the indifference and laziness often observed by teachers and parents represents an attempt to camouflage deeper feelings of anxiety and discouragement.

Junior and senior high students are pressured from many sides to make good grades. Parents probably yell about this more than anyone else. Why? Many parents know that grades are an important factor in being accepted by a college. The truth of the matter is that many colleges consider factors other than grades. Many colleges and universities accept students with average academic ratings. Even the more exclusive, private schools consider leadership ability, participation in extra-curricular activities, and overall promise of maturity.

The U.S. Office of Education reveals that parental pressure for high grades, especially from ambitious mothers who themselves have not attended college, is the prime cause of bright students cheating in high school. Many of them do not have to cheat; they simply want to please the parents with a *higher* grade. A survey made for the Office of Education revealed that only 25 percent of students who felt no maternal pressure cheat, whereas 54 percent of those brighter students who felt a lot of maternal pressure cheat.

There is a kind of subtle pressure that comes with the wide choice of subjects, activities, and leisure time pursuits. A teacher said that today's students have more diversions than students have had at any other time in history. The need to decide causes pressure, but the school is not to blame.

All of this pressure from a success-oriented society leaves the youth very little choice. He either makes the grade or he drops out.

A student should have the right to fail, as often as it may be necessary. Every boy or girl who leaves school is labeled a failure, and the right to fail is one of the few freedoms that this country does not allow its citizens.

Fred Hechinger in the article, "What Sputnik Did to Our

Schools," (*McCalls,* October, 1967) credits the education-science race with Russia for the unreasonable pressure and extreme competitiveness found in the schools today. He believes that Sputnik sparked a revolution in education from an indulgently relaxed scene to an intense, success-oriented one. "Once a pleasantly entertaining sideshow, the business of going to school, studying and passing examinations has moved to the center of the stage, as if it were not so much a rehearsal for life as a crucial chapter of life itself."

Students react to studying and passing exams as ends in themselves. One guidance director says typical student complaints are: "Classes are filled with busywork." "I don't get a chance for real thinking. I keep on reading textbooks and making out class schedules, but I don't have a chance to find out what I like or what I want." "We don't discuss what we learn. We just learn." "Grades become the goal of education. There must be some other reason to study." [3]

So the church worker with youth is seeking the time and attention of people beset with assignments, tests, projects, and term papers—to say nothing of clubs, sports, plays, and so forth, outside the classroom.

For Christian youth, the world of knowledge-getting may pose some special questions. In our American way of life, church and state are separated. Where the rules are strictly adhered to, the usual practice is for the church to be ignored. Religion is treated as one among many cultural factors. Christianity is mentioned only as a historical fact, one religion among many. When ethical values are taught, the motivation offered is a better society. When social studies examine the ills of society, guilt is inevitably placed upon the social system rather than upon sin. In anthropological studies, man is just *here,* a creature who evolved. Science deals with process and function, rarely with origins or reasons.

The secularization of education has been demanded by separation of church and state. Baptists have been in the lead in demanding that religion as subject matter not be the province of the public-school teacher. The youth worker, however, sees special opportunities to relate to the public school learning experiences of Youth.

The quality of public school education is ever increasing. New math is resulting in the faster development of students' minds. Foreign languages are easier to learn due to new methods and earlier beginning of the studies. More and more graduates are able to compete on the college level.

Size of class seems to have a great deal to do with a student's ability to learn. I. M. Scott Elementary School, in San Francisco, maintains small classes. Eighty-five percent of the students are Negro. The school building is old and not modern. Yet the school leads the city in reading achievement. Due to smaller classes, individual attention is more satisfactory.

College Is Not for Everyone

A critical area of education, however, is vocational guidance. Schools are designed to prepare youth to attend college. Often, the youth who decides to attend a technical high school is looked upon as only a step above a dropout. Vocational preparation has not kept pace with college preparatory courses. As a result, the student who is not grade- or college-oriented has less of an opportunity to develop his potentials. Youth workers need to be aware of the difficulty for these youth to find satisfactory lives for themselves and provide vocational guidance retreats of whatever other method seems to speak to the problem. Only about half of the high school graduates will attend college, and perhaps less than half will remain in college until graduation. Churches, then, need to develop an emphasis on the value of labor and of the trades, and use their opportunities to guide youth to feel God's leadership in these areas, as well as those areas which require higher education.

A. Bruce Hawk, superintendent of the Lancaster (Calif.) School District is quoted, "A larger percentage than ever before seem to be finishing high school. I think pressure in high schools is greater than ever—and I think that's wrong. I think that the problem with drugs and liquor among school children around the country is caused in part by the ever-growing pressures on students."

The user may be seeking either a thrill, acceptance and approval, escape from reality, emotional warmth, new and different sensations, cover-up for guilt of past offences, escape from loneliness, relief from responsibility, or an alternative to growing up.

Some are trying to find their limits to their freedom and behavior. Those who find no limitations imposed about them become even more frustrated.

The Student's Search for Identity

Though the design and result is and was not intentional, schools are designed to force all students to respond alike. The result is a loss of the ability to respond creatively, spontaneously. Consequently, the pressures on a young person who is struggling to find a self-image are heavy. Rather than aiding him is his search, the design and structure of public education actually retards him. To be sure, a youth can find his identity in the junior high and high school years. Schools provide a variety of subjects—some required, some elective. Through exposing himself to as wide a variety of subjects as possible, and by involving himself in as many extra-curricular activities as possible, the youth can eventually eliminate some possible talents or interests and develop others. However, the structure of the search makes the task quite difficult.

This examination is not designed to disparage the school system—educators themselves spend a great deal of time doing that in efforts to improve—but to point up the difficulty youth have in their searches for identity. The public school system influences their development tremendously. The youth who has not kept up in his learning to relate to other persons is at a distinct disadvantage. Due to the structure of the system of education, the slow developer, slow learner, or youth who is slow to develop socially is handicapped with increasing intensity as the months and years go by.

A second difficulty with the school system is that it fails to lead the student to develop concern for others. It is primarily self-centered in its structure. That is, choices of curriculum, extra-curricular activities, and interpersonal relationships are primarily made on a basis of meaning to self.

It is estimated that the traditional IQ tests measure only about a fifth of the dimensions of the mind. The potential creativity of the other four-fifths is relatively unexplored. This fact points up the increasing opportunity and responsibility of the churches to attempt to offer opportunities for youth to develop their creative potentials. Again, the fact related here demonstrates the difficulty of the youth to find his full potential. Indeed, since the task is so profound and difficult, the churches may supply the answer through Christ. Rather than the last statement being regarded as a cliche, it should be thoroughly considered in light of the creative power of God. Promises such as inherent in the Baptist doctrine of the priesthood of the believer offer great hope that if churches spoke to the needs of youth to find their full potentials, they would be able to do so in context with God's purposes.

Other studies have indicated the importance of a healthy view of self to learning. The youth who has confidence in himself, who sees himself as a person of worth, who sees himself positively is better able to learn. He brings himself to the learning experience with confidence and so is better assured that he will do the right thing. Lack of confidence blocks the thinking processes and focuses attention of the youth's feeling that he cannot accomplish his goal rather than freeing his spirit to pursue the goal. Such information as this demonstrates the importance of workers with youth to try to find areas in which youth who lack self-confidence can express themselves, can work through their difficulties and hang-ups, can discuss problems with adults, and can learn to relate to other youth—all in order to develop their confidence in themselves.

From a practical standpoint, the worker makes a genuine contribution to Youth when he simply understands the studenthood aspect of life. Some adults understand because they are public-school teachers or because they have teen-agers of their own. Many workers will have to make opportunities to visit nearby high schools, to attend games and plays, and to look over textbooks.

Only with such understanding can a teacher help Youth relate Christian truth to life needs.

Tobacco, Drugs, Liquor

It is impossible to get a complete picture of junior or senior high students without acknowledging the impact tobacco, drugs, and liquor have upon them.

Each year, billions of sedatives and pep pills are diverted to illegal use and ultimate misuse. According to the Food and Drug Administration, this flow produces enough pills or tablets per person per year to "keep everyone in the United States awake and jumping for a week, and enough barbiturates to keep them in a stupor for a week." [4]

The drug scene is a part of a larger one. For years, Americans have been swallowing billions of pills and capsules, including tranquilizers. The American society tolerates alcohol and nicotine, both of which technically are drugs.

The authors do not intend, however, to try to prove the volume of use, to use scare tactics, nor even to debate the harmful effects of tobacco, alcohol, or drugs. But youth workers need to be aware that all three are used to some degree in most groupings of the youth culture—a culture which does not usually pronounce harsh judgments upon them for the use of one or more of these.

Some church youth arrive late at a church meeting "leaning on a cigarette" for support. They may have to leave during the meeting to give additional boosts to their sagging egos from a package, can, or bottle. Therefore, it cannot be surprising that some of them find the need for stronger stuff as they bluster their confused way from thrill to thrill. They are afraid the thrill-go-round will stop and they may find themselves at their own doors ... still, quiet, alone; and what is worse, conscious of their loneliness. Some of them are very lonely, even in a noisy crowd.

A quiet, well-mannered, easily-influenced and anxious young person may sense that his weak personality cannot stand the jolts and knocks of a hard-fisted socio-economic order. So, he may anesthetize his sensitive self with cigarettes, booze, or pot. Others live some of their hours in an acceptable straight life while spending many hours in a fantasy world of dolls and toys and harsh judgments; all of which tend to isolate them from their peers. However, if a youth builds his fantasy world by smoking and drinking and experimenting with drugs he can be acceptable to many of his peers.

The user may be seeking a thrill, acceptance and approval, escape from reality, emotional warmth, new and different sensations, cover-up for guilt of past offences, escape from loneliness, relief from responsibility, or an alternative to growing up. All of them are trying to find the limits to their freedom and behavior. Those who find no limitations imposed on them become even more frustrated. These youth desperately need approval, not of their actions, but as struggling persons. They need acceptance, not because of their habits, but in spite of them.

Youth workers and parents need to follow sound principles in their efforts to help youth who have problems with the use and abuse of drugs. These suggestions may be helpful:

1. Don't try to force emotionally charged opinions on the students.
2. Don't generalize with exaggerated statements which cannot be supported by reliable information.
3. Treat seriously with as little shock as possible any information you may learn about a youth's interest in drugs.
4. Remember that the primary concern is for the welfare of a certain boy or girl, not reaction against a drug.

5. Cooperate with your local school in any educational projects they sponsor on the use or abuse of drugs.

The youth worker who understands studenthood works creatively with the questioning mind of youth, encourages him to do his best at school, and helps him to deeper faith in the living God.

The worker with Youth can never really "get through" to those with whom he works until he understands fully the meaning and importance of studenthood. It is not easy, perhaps, for the earnest church worker to accept the fact that the hours at church, which are so important to him, catch a minor part of the attention of the Youth. Workers must always work with pull from two directions: first, the desire to have time and attention of the Youth so that they can provide the most meaningful church experiences possible; and second, the realization that school life is highly important, demanding maximum time and attention.

Some adults understand the studenthood aspect of a Youth's life because they have teen-agers of their own. Many workers will have to *make opportunities* to visit nearby high schools, to attend games and plays, and to become acquainted with the student's textbooks and reading matter.

1. E. Z. Friedenberg, *Coming of Age in America* (New York: Random House, 1965), p. 49.

2. Ruth Strang, *The Adolescent Views Himself* (New York: McGraw-Hill Book Co., Inc., 1957), p. 257.

3. Harry Smallenburg, "Pressures on Students—A Guidance Director's Viewpoint," *National Education Association*, September, 1966, pp. 28-29.

4. Alton Blakeslee, "Safeguarding Your Teen-Ager Against Harmful Drugs," *Maryville-Alcoa Times*, AP, March 10, 1969, p. 10.

Chapter 9. WHERE HAVE ALL
THE OTHERS GONE?

MY LIFE AS A SIDEWALK
by D. M., age 14

One day, it was one of those hot summer days. I was laying
down beside the street and I did not tell you that I was a
sidewalk. It was on a Saturday. I cannot remember if it
was in the morning or the afternoon. So let me get to the
story now.

Everybody was busy walking on me and I was trying to
get a sun tan. I was very mad. I almost started to blow the
people off, but I started to think of the people that made me
a sidewalk. So I said to myself in the night I will get my
suntan. But then I realized that when the sun goes down
you can't get a tan.

Then I blew the people off of me and from then on they
did not walk on me again and I got my suntan at last.[1]

These words came from a teen-ager who lives in the ghetto
of New York City's east side.

But not all the disadvantaged children live in what we call
ghettoes. Not all school drop-outs live in poverty. There are
social drop-outs and social pushed-outs. There are emotionally-
starved adolescents who lash out at the society which they be-

lieve deprives them of this love by becoming anti-social, even destructive. There are teens—living in the best houses in the best sections of villages or cities—who are neglected or even rejected by parents, peers, and even Christian youth leaders.

Where have all these others gone? Those who don't fit the mold of the nice, good, all-American teen-age image?

The writers saw a seventeen-year-old girl working at the lunch counter of a local drug store during school hours. It was her second day at work. She had, in fact, dropped out of the eleventh grade several weeks earlier. She was a normal girl who attended football games like most girls. As the conversation progressed, she said, "Oh, I don't know why I quit . . . Yes, I do know. I quit because I'm nervous." And, to her, this seemed to be a satisfactory explanation.

Former Vice President Hubert H. Humphrey said that in the fall of 1967 almost 1,000,000 students did not return to the classrooms.

The best available estimate is that one third of all youth will never finish high school. One authority says that 40 per cent will drop out. Contrary to popular beliefs, these drop-outs are not all from lower class, lower income families.

Who Is the Dropout?

Edgar Z. Friedenberg gives an excellent description of some dropouts:

> They are ill-disciplines. They have no basic skills. They are so sore that any place you touch them hurts; and when they are hurt, they hurt back. They are extremely parochial, limited in their experiences of the world to a few city blocks of desolate slum, and therefore, both gullible and suspicious about anything beyond it. They are sometimes homeless; they never have any quiet place to study and think. They are inconveniently aware of their own sexuality and inconveniently skilled at bringing it to the attention of others. They live, their teachers sometimes say, like animals; and as they say it, a ghost sobs, harshly.[2]

Dr. Friedenberg goes on to say that many of them hate the

noise, the filth, the crowding, the vulnerability to the police, the illness. But they also resent the mass media, including the school, telling them that if they were any good at all they would be middle class like everybody else and live in a nice house in a quiet subdivision. "But the fact that they have reason to hate their life of fear and deprivation does not give us the right to force ours on them as the only acceptable alternative to it. This is something they must work out for themselves; the school's job is to help them understand most fully the meaning and nature of what they have to work with." [3]

Paul Goodman reminds us that there is another kind of dropout—the "stay-in-school" dropouts—those who stay in school but who drop out internally: the daydreamer; the one who has lost aspiration and imagination; the one who feels his liberty caged or scheduled. Most of these are from the middle class, and most of them have the ability to get tuned in . . . *if*.

Many dropouts (from school, church, and social activities) have personality disorders. These come from all classes of society. John H. Rohrer says these disorders often develop in the young adolescent who has grown to mistrust individuals; who has had no significant adult figure to offer him emotional support; who has had to turn to peer groups to find someone to relate to emotionally; who has become frustrated and strikes back at the sources of frustration, whether it is authority figures or peer groups who have snubbed him. It might also be one who was forced to depend too much upon maternal figures. It might be one who was seeking in an inadequate manner ways of satisfying his need for affection and emotional warmth. In this connection, Rohrer says that this seeking for affection explains the large frequency of dropouts due to teen-age pregnancies. "In the vast majority of the cases the pregnancy is not the result of sheer lust but an attempt to get emotional warmth and 'closeness' from a second individual." [4]

Why Do They Drop Out?

Most students who drop out of school feel that they are not

wanted there. Dr. Duvall says that many students simply "keel over" or wither under the impact of rejection stacked upon rejection until they actually begin to feel like rejects.

The adolescent who drops out of school has usually dropped out socially earlier. It was discovered that more than two thirds of Maryland's dropouts had never participated in athletics or any other extra-class activities.

Lack of parental encouragement is also a factor. The low income child usually comes from homes where the parents are poorly educated. He does not have books, magazines, nor any of the other study aids which most children have. When the teacher makes an assignment predicated upon the student's access to these items away from the class room, the economically deprived child is left out in the cold. His parents have not taught him how to dress, and there is no money for clothes, anyway. The parents have not taught him common manners and social graces, because they themselves do not know them. The parents may not be able to provide proper medical care; nor do they know where to seek free care. Some children need glasses. Many families live in one or two rooms so that there is no quiet, private place to study.

Many native-born children experience conflicts with their foreign-born parents. Schools sometimes intensify this parent-youth conflict by encouraging the student to reject the cultural values of their parents.

Dr. Duvall says that one of the saddest aspects of the culturally disadvantaged youth is the tight little life space he has to call his own. His experience is too narrow to let him know what life is all about beyond his own little gang. His scope is so limited that he often does not even know what the teacher nor the textbook is trying to say. He has so few experiences to build upon—and the experiences he has had are not used in his learning activities. You can shut a human being out of society just so long. When he finds nothing to relate to, no one who even tries to understand him, he is going to build a world of his own . . . somewhere . . . with someone . . . for better or for worse.

E. V. Kohrs says that another factor in the adolescent's decision to drop out is that public education is permeated with middle-class values which are foreign to the lower class student. The lower class adolescent brings his parental values with him and is penalized and rejected. His behavior is not morally acceptable. He may not be deliberately breaking rules. He may be acting and reacting in the only way he knows to be right— which, of course, turns out to be wrong. In an effort to escape these pressures, he withdraws from school.

Strang says that the students who drop out when they definitely have the ability to stay in leave because they dislike the program, the methods of teaching, the teachers, or because they feel unable to learn some required subject. There are some who could make it academically but leave to help make a living for their families or to get married.

Some drop out or freak out in order to escape a challenge, a commitment. This escape permits the youth the luxury of retiring as an undefeated champion. Quite often, a boy will acquire the reputation of being able to bully his way through any situation or of passing without studying. If he comes upon a situation where he has to commit himself in a way that will cause him to loose his reputation, he may take retirement as the easy way out.

Cottle makes a rather startling statement about another kind of freak out. He says that the accomplishments by so many are so great, the knowledge and awareness so swift in coming and so deep in meaning, that society leaves youth with no excuse for failure other than severe illness or total collapse.

Poverty and drop-outs do not always go together. There are exceptions. Dr. Duvall maintains that most of the time when a child living in poverty succeeds, he has at least one parent or one teacher who *cared* about him, encouraged him to go as far and as fast as his abilities would permit. There is a difference in being poor with parents who are able to encourage a youth— who have faith in their child and faith in God, who have contact with the outside world, who care. There is quite a difference in this kind of struggle for an education and in being poor with parents who trust no one, God included; who don't care what you do as long as you stay out of the house; who, if they ever had a dream of anything better, have long since given up in utter despair; who have been very few blocks from the dirty rat-infested places called home.

"One difference between the urban slum today and that of decades ago is that so many families now have been in a culture of poverty so long that they no longer have dreams for their children's futures. The immigrant family may have been desperately poor in money and goods, but it had high hopes for its sons and daughters, and inspired many a young person to grow up and out." [5] Sam Levenson is a good example. He tells about the poverty of his immigrant parents as they raised a large family in New York City. *But they had a vision for their children.*

Is There Any Hope?

Strang acknowledges that it is difficult to help the socially rejected adolescent. Superficial reassurance urging him to join a club or go to a party may only make him feel his social inadequacy all the more. Nothing can be accomplished without trying to understand the cause of his isolation.

It is almost impossible to help the disadvantaged and rejected teen-ager unless there is some basic, logical reason to establish a *continuing* relationship. In other words, a worker can't just walk down into the middle of a group of socially or economically disadvantaged teen-agers and say, "Look, I'm here. Come and let me help you." There needs to be a meeting ground which preserves the dignity of the individual. Some church groups have worked with schools to tutor students on a one-to-one basis. Other youth leaders work in the Girls' Club or Boys' Club in order to find this meeting ground. Some churches open their recreation programs to all individuals in the community—not just their members—and the regular workers with Youth help with these programs.

The sad facts are that these teens are not frequenting church schools and they are not likely to. But there is no way to escape the Christian responsibility for these persons.

Jesus inaugurated his public ministry by telling the people in the synagogue what he was about. He read from the prophet:

> The Spirit of the Lord is upon me:
> for he has consecrated me to preach the gospel
>   to the poor,
> he has sent me to proclaim release for captives
>   and recovery of sight for the blind,
> to set free the oppressed,
>   to proclaim the Lord's year of favour.
>   —*Luke 4: 18-19, Moffatt* [6]

Jesus said very plainly that his people are to be about the same business. Can churches find ways to meet the needs of this large segment of teen-age society?

Nina Brereton wrote a sad, revealing article entitled, "I Hurt! I Hurt! I Hurt!" (*Seventeen*, February, 1969) She was not economically deprived. She enrolled in an academically and socially prestigious girls' school when she was in the seventh grade, but she said that the first year there was only one girl who would come home and eat potato chips with her after school. Because of this rejection, she decided to rebel. She said, "My purpose was to create a groovy, detached image of myself and to show the kids at school that I really had better things to do than be with them (which was a lie). I started messing around with a lot of different boys, not because I liked them so much but because I loved to feel somebody's arms around me, to feel wanted." [7]

At fourteen, she began "turning on" with pot, hashish, and pills. Later she "tripped" quite often with *LSD*. She hung around with other acid heads.

She wrote the article for *Seventeen* to tell about the organization, *Encounter, Inc.*, a nonresidential drug rehabilitation program run by ex-addicts with the help of social workers for the teen-age preaddicts. Here she was able to find out *why* she relied on drugs. After sitting in a group therapy session and screaming to the top of her voice, for dozens of times, the words "I hurt," this lonely sixteen-year-old girl found out about herself.

> "I guess you know what you need now," someone said.
> I laughed again and said, "Yeah, I guess so."
> "What is it?" he said. I knew the answer of course; it was just that the words were hard.
> "I need . . . I need love," I said.

She said that she never felt the need to get high again, "because I'm getting what I need, and when I don't, I ask for it. [She told of asking her mother to hold her and tell her she loved her.] Now I know I need love, lots of it, shown in physical, tangible ways from lots of people, men and women alike—and so do you." [8]

There are many youth in homes, schools, and churches who inwardly cry, *I hurt! I hurt! I hurt!* but who are not secure enough to verbalize the hard-to-say words, *I need . . . I need love.*

> And . . . God is love
> and we are trying to do his work
> of loving one another
> and bearing each other's burden
> and caring for those who hurt
> and need love.

1. Stephen M. Joseph, *The Me Nobody Knows: Children's Voices from the Ghetto* (New York: Avon Books, 1969), p. 132.

2. Daniel Schreiber, editor, *The School Dropout*, Project: School Dropouts National Education Association, Washington, p. 37.

3. *Ibid.*, p. 37.

4. *Ibid.*, p. 38.

5. Evelyn Duvall, *Today's Teen-Agers* (New York: Association Press, 1966), p. 66.

6. From: The Bible: A New Translation, by James Moffatt. Copyright 1950 by James Moffatt. Reprinted by permission of Harper & Row, Publishers, Inc.

7. Nina Brereton, "I Hurt! I Hurt! I Hurt!" *Seventeen*, Vol. XXVIII, No. 2, Feb., 1969, pp. 144 ff.

8. *Ibid.*, pp. 212, 214.

PART 3

Youth's Values and Involvement

God knows I'm searching for something.
But what?...
There is a void inside me
    that cries out to be filled.

Chapter 10. WHERE THE ACTION IS

One twelve-year-old was asked at school to do something which, to the rest of the class, seemed like a routine assignment. She was asked to answer this question: *If you could wish three wishes which you knew would come true, what would you wish?* The rest of the class dashed off three wishes in the allotted time, but one girl asked the teacher for more time to think.

Later she told her mother about it. "First," she said, "I wished that there would be no more war. Second, I wished that everyone in the world could have a house to live in with plenty of food to eat and clothes to wear. I am afraid that I was a little selfish with my last wish. It was just for me."

The mother braced herself for the typical I-wish-I-had-a-million-dollars wish. Instead, the daughter said, "I wished that I could have as my very own any book in the whole world that I wanted to read."

Youth are altruistic. Even the younger ones are concerned with world peace. Dr. Knight says this concern may be due in part to a yearning for peace within themselves. "Through the mental mechanism of projecting his inner turmoil onto the outer world, his yearning for peace within himself may take the form of a wish for world peace and social accord. Upheaval in the outer world intensifies his inner conflict, for he needs the steadying influence of moral strength and unity in the world around him." [1]

He may take as his ideal the religious man who fights for social justice. He needs attractive young adults as models—adults who are concerned with public morality involving such issues as war, hunger, poverty, ignorance, population explosion, etc.

Youth are discontented with the world as it now is. A part of their discontented search and native exuberance is, according to Eric Erikson, the craving for *locomotion*. This craving may be expressed in a general desire to be constantly on the go—a characteristic partly due to the fact that the practice of moving about is established as a way of life early in youth's development.

Discontent may also be expressed in vigorous work, sports, racing, or constant activity. "But it also finds expression," says Eric Erikson, "through participation in the movements of the day (whether the riots of a local commotion or the parades and campaigns of major ideological forces), if they only appeal to the need for feeling moved and for feeling essential in moving something along toward an open future." [2]

But there is a difference between youth's ideal, altruistic wishes and their involvement in the nitty-gritty issues of the day. Let's consider, for example, how they use most of their spare time. What are they really doing?

Accompanied by Music

Music is an integral part of life for practically all teen-agers. In 1956, a twenty-one-year-old singer from Memphis gyrated into the consciousness of American youth singing "Heartbreak Hotel." Elvis Presley, sporting long sideburns, skin-tight pants, and an electric guitar, rode to fame—bumping, writhing, and selling.

In 1969 he had sold 200 million recordings. He had developed into one of the most vital forces in American pop culture. "He has had more impact on popular American music in the past ten years than any other single personality. It was he who began the contemporary revolution in musical taste, inspired the Beatles and most other singers. Thanks to him, 80 percent of the singles and 50 percent of all record albums are purchased by youngsters under the age of 25." [3]

According to a recent study made by the Bank of California, rock music will leap from a $5 million to a $15 million enterprise within the next ten years.

Adults may protest rock music on one of several grounds. Teens may actually suffer a hearing loss from its piercing loud sounds. But music (right now, *rock* and *soul*) is an inseparable part of teen-age land. There is absolutely no way youth can be understood apart from their music. Adults don't have to like it, but they need to understand why youth like it.

Burt Korall says that if anything is true of contemporary popular music, "it is the intent of its makers to set life to music . . . Politics, sexuality, racial pride, deep and true feelings have entered popular music to stay." [4] It is no longer possible, he asserts, to separate music and life as it really is.

There is another part of life mirrored in the lonely sounds. It is no accident that so many of the songs of youth *are* lonely sounds. Many of their dances express their loneliness. Prewett says their "dances have evolved to the point where two lonesome people jig on a crowded floor in their lonesome ways, neither touching nor many times seeing each other." [5] If the 70's bring a change in style, the change will reflect life.

For adults to respond negatively to the music of youth as if it were an affront to the soul and senses serves no good purpose. Charles W. Keysor, a Methodist pastor in Elgin, Illinois, says, "We have to hear the loneliness, the despair, the awful futility and triviality of which popular music is but a symptom. 'Pop' music may be God's way of telling us how desperately millions of people need Jesus Christ." [6]

Burt Korall looks on the pop music as youth taking the pulse of the world as well as their own pulse; using music to purge themselves, while increasingly irritating and provoking the forces of reaction.

In the early months of 1969, the pop music took on a more affirmative tone. The songs begin to define what *might be*—what could be, as opposed to merely expressing a condition. This development must reveal at least a sign of hope on youth's part, because music is a commentary on how they assess the times. Parents and adult Youth workers would do well to remember that the songs are written by young adults—persons over twenty and some over thirty—but they are bought and sung by youth. Perhaps the songwriters are able to listen to the heartbeat of youth better than most adults. Or, perhaps they simply are more willing to listen, even though for the money involved.

Since adults have different needs than Youth, they cannot thoroughly identify and find satisfaction in the music of young people; but the experience of listening will be educational. Adult workers might turn loose and let the emotion of the music surge through their minds and bodies, without trying to take every word, phrase, or idea in the text too literally. The youth may not agree with all the plaintive pleadings for love, but he knows he needs love in a more mature form than he has known during childhood. He may not agree with the hopelessness and despair expressed in many of the songs, but he probably has personally experienced some of these feelings and therefore identifies with them as a real part of his life. He may not actively agree with cloudy expressions of "belief," but he may be equally discontent with some concepts of God taught and preached at church.

Sight and Sound

The reading habits of youth vary from one section of the country to another, and even from one youth to another. Most junior and senior high students do not have time during the school year to read very much of anything merely for pleasure.

Some of them do read magazines. Their assigned reading list is about all most of them can handle.

A local check with school librarians revealed that these are the most read magazines in the library: *Sports Illustrated* and *Outdoor Life* for boys. *Seventeen* and *Good Housekeeping* for girls. Other popular magazines are: For boys, *Flying, Electronics World, Sports Afield, Popular Mechanics, Car and Driver;* for girls, *Better Homes and Gardens, Teen, Co-Ed, Glamour, McCalls, Ingenue, Redbook;* read by both boys and girls, *Holiday, Readers' Digest, World Tennis, Newsweek, Look, Time, Ebony, Life.*

The high school libraries in this section did not subscribe to *Playboy* nor *Cosmopolitan*, although they are both available on the newsstands. According to the salespeople, they are purchased more by college students than high school students.

What about movies? Of all movie goers, 11 percent are under age sixteen, 41 percent are between the ages of sixteen and twenty-four (figures from 1968). It is impossible to know what movies teens see, but in all likelihood, high school teens simply see whatever appears at the major movie houses in their towns or cities. If the teens are going out, either on a date or just with a group of their own sex, the movie is still the most accessible, first-thought-of entertainment. The movies are discussed. If a movie is a topic of conversation, youth wants to see it. Another factor which adds to the popularity of the movie theater is that it is a class leveler. Anyone can go, and all are equals there. An additional reason for the popularity of movies for dating is that they provide an easy-way-out kind of entertainment.

Youth will not allow adults (except parents—sometimes) to censor their choices, but they might allow adult workers to help them evaluate movies. *The Graduate* was perhaps the most talked about movie in the late 1960's. One boy said he saw the film with his parents and then went home and had a long talk about morals with them. He said, "It was the first time we had been able to communicate on that level. I enjoyed the talk." [7]

Older Youth's Concern with War, Poverty, and Social Justice

Youth have heard the figures that millions of Americans suffer periodically from hunger and some malnutrition. They also know that if children go hungry at certain crucial ages, they may suffer brain damage that can never be repaired.

Youth know that chemical and biological weapons are waiting to destroy persons. Life is sacred for Youth.

Youth know that the draft (compulsory military conscription) is fast becoming a permanent American institution. It has been around for twenty-eight years. The boys are torn between loyalty to their country and a desire to be able to plan their lives without this interruption.

Youth are very much aware of the social injustice found in our nation and the whole world.

Youth are aware of the population explosion—bringing more and more children into these poverty pockets where children and adults are already starving.

What can they do about such big, life-sapping, life-taking problems? Not much, they feel. But they know that the problem will not go away. They still see it. They cannot watch the evening news without seeing men killed. They cannot read the morning paper without glaring at the statistics of starving children. They cannot ride through certain sections of town without being aware of improper housing and abject poverty. The problems remain. They want to change the situations, but what can they do?

There are a few youth here and there who do get involved in these major issues, but according to Gordon, on the whole even late adolescents do not want to get wrapped up in social issues. Youth questions whether he really is his brother's keeper. Gordon also says that "it is difficult for the adolescent to solve his conflicts in regard to social morality in a society that is itself conflicted." [8]

But what about those who are involved? What are they doing? Volunteers are working in hospitals, tutoring slum children, assisting in adult education, raising money for charity work, helping in disaster areas, serving in the poverty programs, working in political campaigns, teaching in summer day care centers.

As with adults, so with youth, it is easier to be committed to a principle than it is to work toward carrying out that principle. It is easier to give assent to a national political figure who embodies those ideals than it is to try to accomplish those ideals on the local level. Sylvie Reice, youth editor of *McCalls*, wrote an editorial in the November, 1968, issue called, "Quo Vadis, Youth?" She appealed to youth not to drop out of politics just because they had been disillusioned, but to shift their energies to a new and vital area of operation—the local scene.

Race relations is one area where older youth (post high school) are working on the local scene. He sees a new religious element emerging which embraces the promise of a mankind freer of the attitudes of a species which thinks it is bigger and better than any other species.

Youth are action oriented. They want to see constructive and immediate results. They want constructive changes.

1. Gene Usdin, M.D., editor, *Adolescence: Care and Counseling* (Philadelphia: J. B. Lippincott Co., 1967), p. 44.

2. Eric H. Erikson, *Identity, Youth and Crisis* (New York: W. W. Norton, 1968), p. 243.

3. Derek Norcross, "The Influence of Elvis Presley," *Parade* Sunday Supplement, February 9, 1969, p. 27.

4. Burt Korall, "The Music of Protest," *Saturday Review*, November 16, 1968, pp. 37-38.

5. David Prewett, "Contemporary Youth and Family Relationships: The Alienated and Their Families," *Southern Baptist Family Life Education*, January-March, 1968, p. 2.

6. Charles W. Keysor, "What Is Pop Music Really Saying?" *Christianity Today*, 1966.

7. Bob Thomas, "How Teen-Agers Feel About Modern Films," *Knoxville News Sentinel*, March 2, 1969, p. F9.

8. Ira J. Gordon, *Human Development: From Birth Through Adolescence* (New York: Harper, 1962), p. 364.

Chapter 11. IN THE BEGINNING GOD

• A teen-age boy said, "I simply cannot accept Jesus as anything but a plain, mortal, normal man. I have alienated myself from the entire mystical concept of Christianity. I have no faith in anything but myself."

• A class of sixteen-year-old girls listened politely, silently as the frustrated teacher tried to explain the Holy Spirit. Finally, one girl who had been in the church all of her life replied, "Mrs. Westmore, we don't want to hurt your feelings, but we don't have the slightest idea what you're talking about. We believe in God, but why do you have to waste your time trying to convince us that there is some kind of *hocus pocus* about it all. Frankly, this has no meaning at all for my life."

• Some youth shout openly, "I'm a rebel." Bob Oldenburg permits a youth to hurl these words at their religious counterparts in the musical *Good News:*

> You can sing your hymns and pray,—
> I out-grew them yesterday!—

They just sorta cramp my plans;—
Gotta be free, you know, live loose, man!

I'm a rebel! That's me man!
I'm a rebel! Yes, I am!
It doesn't matter what you say,—
'Cause I'll be headed in the other way! [1]

• Some of the same teens who shout, "I'm a rebel" will on other occasions affirm, "There is a God." A seventeen-year-old boy said it like this:

> We face
> > Troubles, trials, temptations,
> > Anguish, anxiety,
> > Sorrow, sin, sickness
> > Death . . .
> > And there is God.
> We find
> > Happiness, joy, friendship,
> > Success, wealth,
> > Love, life, forgiveness,
> > Peace . . .
> > And *there* is God.
> > > —*Andy Morton*

• Underneath all the shouts, there is a longing to experience God in the inner being of most youth. A character in the play *The Mask* expressed her need for God like this: "God, how do I come to you? There is a void inside me that cries out to be filled. I believe you can fill it, but how do I find you?" [2]

• A young man expressed his longings in a similar fashion: "God knows I'm searching for something. But what? I've never seen the Lord. Has anyone? What good would it do to look for him? Where would I find him? Why doesn't someone *show* me God instead of telling me to look for him?" [3]

Adolescent Religion

Religion is not something separate and removed from life. It is a part of life itself. If religion is to be understood and accepted, it must be experienced. It must be more than doctrine and dogma; it must be a living experience. Religious truth must be seen by adolescents to be true in their own contemporary experiences.

"Religious growth is not something separate from the rest of the child's development. It is an interpretation of all his experiences, which he relates to what he believes to be the nature of the divine.[4]

Until religion becomes a part of the teen's experience, it may be nothing more than mere religious vocabulary. The "language of Zion" does not communicate very well, certainly not with youth. Many adults have separated religion from life—put their beliefs off in a corner, neatly sorted, filed and stacked, card indexed and computerized; so that they need only to pull the right card, or press the right button, or quote the right chapter and verse when proof of "rightness" is needed. A good exercise in frustration would be to explain to someone—without referring to personal experience—in down-to-earth, non-theological terms what "saved by grace through faith" means. Such an experiment emphasizes the importance of *experience* to doctrinal understanding.

This problem is not new. In *The Pilgrim's Progress,* Christian said to Talkative: "Religion hath no place in his heart, or house, or conversation: all that he hath lieth in his tongue, and his religion is to make a noise therewith."[5]

For the most part, teens have tolerated this "respectable religion." Stewart says that many of them accept religion because it is an easy way to conform with parents or the teen group. In most sections of middle-class America, it would be the exception for the youth *not* to be affiliated in some way with a church.

This affiliation, of course, does not mean the same thing to all youth. For some, faith is a freeing experience. For others, it is restrictive. For some, it is a creative opening to the outside world. For others, it is a withdrawal from the world. For others, it is a form of conformity. The same characteristics are true with adults, of course.

The kind of culture the youth finds himself in today directly influences the kinds of experiences he will undergo with respect to the church and religious beliefs.

Some youth turn to religion to provide consolation and a sense of identity. A young person looked back on her teen years of faithful church activism and said: "I know now that I went to church every time the doors were opened, taught mission Sunday School, and became known as "good" not because I was living out *experienced* Christianity but because I needed the praise and love of the church leaders. You see, I never felt loved at home, so I thought I could *buy* the love and admiration of the pastor and church leaders by 'being good.' "

Much Christian Youth work is an attempt to shield Youth from the world around them, to make them into something like super-youth who are different, distinguished, free from frustration, and great masters of life. To reach Youth with the tremendous message of the gospel, they need to become aware that God is at work in the *world* and in their lives—and not just in the church with the good kids.

One adult expressed the result of the kind of appeal to Youth which does not really relate the gospel message to life, but which rather challenges Youth to live in an unreal church-world:

> I learned well what I *thought* the church had been teaching me since I was a teen-ager: God loved me when I was good. As a young person, I lived with this by trying to be "good" —a super-youth who was better and greater than those around me. I didn't do *this* and I didn't do *that* and I *did* go to church and literally devoured the doctrines of "What Baptists Believe." And, I felt that God loved me. But do you know, there came a day of reckoning, personally, for me. A day when I had to face myself and my motivations, and I knew that if God loved me when I was good, he must *not* love me when I was not good. So I passed through dark days, and months, and years feeling unloved by God, because I knew that there was so little good in me. But then in an unmistakable way, I discovered that God loved *all* of me. He loved me when I was good. He loved me when I was bad. As Gertrude Behanna would say: *God happened to me* and I knew he loved me . . . and all other persons

whether they were good or bad, like me or different from me, rich or poor, yellow or black.

Youth need to *experience* God in their lives—*in the world where they live*—not just learn *about* him. In order to accomplish such an educational task, they need freedom to think things out for themselves. Goldman says, "What stands out more than anything else is the desire of most adolescents to think for themselves. Since religion is ultimately a personal encounter with truth we should welcome rather than oppose such a desire." [6]

Stewart, in *Adolescent Religion,* said that whether a young adolescent begins to think abstractly and how he does depends among other things upon the permission of his parents and religious leaders to engage in such thinking, questioning, and doubting, and upon the development of a viewpoint around which he can cluster his thoughts.

The adolescent is going to find something—some philosophy, some goal, some god—to give himself to. "The individual self will either be unified in love and faith in the living God—or it will seek unity by giving itself away to the false gods so abundant today." [7]

Concepts of God and the Church

Dr. Knight of Tulane University interviewed prospective pre-med students regarding their ideas of religious conflicts experienced during middle adolescence. Most of them said they had built their belief-system around a single pillar—belief in God—but not many expressed any great need for the institutional church as important or essential to their religion.

Goldman tells of an eighteen-year-old who said he believed firmly in God, in Christ as Saviour, and in the role of the church in society, but said: "I'm bored by a lot of churchiness, and some of our preachers seem a hundred years out of date." [8]

Youth also object to the kind of Bible study which seeks to protect them from problems such as seeming conflicts in Scripture and problems of interpretation. They feel unprepared to face these problems later in life—as they undoubtedly will have to do.

Stewart concluded from a survey he made that although the largest number of youth accept the forms and systems of their churches without question, they felt an emotional distance from God, and they did a poor job of intergrating their beliefs into their way of living. Many youth attend church, church school, and youth groups for purely utilitarian reasons.

A psychiatrist who worked with Goldman on the Normal Development Project felt that most of the young people observed in this project were living on values fed them by their parents— that they had not experienced firsthand struggle with religious realities such as sin, guilt, forgiveness, faith, and commitment. He felt that the adolescents paid lip service to the articles of belief but that their real loyalties were to group values.

Why is this lack of depth in religion a characteristic? Why all the meaningless lip service? Are Youth afraid to tell their parents and leaders that church attendance has little or no meaning for them? Are they afraid to admit this even to themselves? Do they need the security of church activities? *Or,* is it possible for them to arrive at a concept of God and the church which is understandable to them? Which has meaning in the experiences and language of their lives?

Some adolescents stop thinking about religion before they consciously reject it, perhaps because they are confused over much of the language used and thoughts expressed in the Bible —language which they do not understand and Hebrew thought patterns which are foreign to them.

Much of the problem is not that youth are so irreligious or unconcerned, but rather that many young people have not gained an understanding of the *language of the Christian faith.* "We need to learn that many young persons will be using unconventional words and actions to express their hungers and needs. In their own way, they witness to the truth of their hope that the gospel is, in fact, a reality at the heart of all things. They may not use the word 'gospel' but they may be talking about the reality of this life of faith and love." [9] Language which has become familiar to adults may mean something quite different (or nothing at all) to Youth. After all, religious terminology was originally chosen because of its *ability to communicate* a truth. That language today which communicates divine truth best, then, is to be sought out and used.

One young person expressed the desire to discover something for herself when she said: "I just don't like the way some ministers get up and yell and scream and everything and I don't think that's necessary. Well, you see again, screaming and everything is by force. It's putting fear into the people and that's just another one of those old tricks. Whereas the way our minister does it, he doesn't put any fear in men, he just instills a want to repent, just because he leads off and you finish up yourself or something." [10]

How Well Is the Church Doing Its Job?

Unfortunately, there is not a great deal of accurate data available to answer this question. In fact, books upon books have been and are still being written on what the church's job is in the first place. Merton Strommen made a survey of Lutheran high-school youth several years ago. Southern Baptists have conducted an extensive youth survey prepared by professional researchers. (A synopsis is printed in the back of this book.)

The book *Growing Up in River City* contains a chapter on "Youth and the Church." The book presents the results of a scientific research study carried on by a group of social scientists from the University of Chicago during the years 1951-1960. The members of the group, from a midwestern city of 45,000, were in the sixth grade (age 11) when the study commenced. The study continued throughout adolescence and terminated when most of the group had reached twenty years of age. The individuals were observed as they played, worked, and studied in the schools, churches, homes, and shops of River City. The researchers felt that the church is "one of the principal institutions for social and personal development of youth in American society—(that) it is expected to have a positive effect over and above that of the family and that of the school." [11]

River City was well churched. It included 32 Protestant churches, 8 Roman Catholic, 1 Jewish, 1 Bahai. Each of the 42 clergymen or responsible leaders of religious groups was enlisted to help gather information and evaluation on the 430 boys and girls in the study. Here are some of their conclusions:

> Boys and girls from families of higher status are far more likely to be seen by the clergy as interested in and active in the church. Boys and girls of greater intelligence, and those who are more successful in school, are also more likely to be active in church. Finally, boys and girls who are better adjusted personally and socially are more likely to be interested in church than are those who are maladjusted . . .
>
> There is certainly no evidence here of the redeeming power of the church in River City. On the other hand, a more intensive study would certainly show that a number (although admittedly a small number) have been greatly helped by the church to overcome handicaps of personal inferiority and social background when home and school were inadequate for them.[12]

There was general agreement among all the researchers on these two points:

1. The church cooperated with the school and home to help the most successful boys and girls grow up well.
2. There is a very large group of boys and girls who are unsuccessful or at the most indifferently successful, with whom the church has no contact at all.

While this study was conducted in a single region, the results should be thoroughly evaluated in light of the results of the recent survey of Southern Baptist youth. (See Appendix B.)

What Can I Believe?

Ready-made religion may impede a child's spiritual growth

"because passively acquired information is more quickly forgotten and ready-made religion is more easily jettisoned than where truth and belief have been the result of personal growth." [13]

As youth develop the power and confidence to think for themselves and to express their disapproval, they also develop the ability to resist dogmatism. This is a hard fact for adult leaders and parents to accept. It is almost as though some adults are afraid to let them ask and seek and knock.

Dr. John Claypool says that in our religious pilgrimage we are to *keep on* asking, *keep on* seeking, *keep on* knocking. He says,

> It astounds me all over again how unsure and unbelieving most Christians are today at this very point of asking and receiving. I know many parents who want to reverse the sequence of Jesus and give the answers to their children before the questions. They want the church to be a kind of hothouse enterprise where doubt is forbidden and their children are given only one alternative. What is so evident in this approach is the insecurity of such indoctrination. If . . . one has never really asked or sought or knocked, but simply taken over cheaply and uncritically what their parents believed or some authority dictated, they are threatened indeed by this approach of 'search unlimited.' It is high time, it seems to me, for the Church to take its Lord seriously and encourage the kind of openness toward truth that enables truth to open to men." [14]

It is not uncommon for an adolescent to enter a stage of agnosticism, especially if he has become disillusioned with his own father or the concept he held of God. One of the learning tasks an adolescent has is to separate his father from God. As he tries to become independent, he may try to declare his freedom from either father or God or both. Many times his "rebellion against religion is often against what he thought was taught him. He is rejecting chiefly his own childhood conceptions, for which he may illogically blame his culture, parents and church. Many years may pass before he realizes that his rebellion was not so much against parents, church or culture as against his own immaturity." [15]

Dr. Ruth Strang says that an antagonistic response to religion may simply be an expression of hostility toward parents and really has little to do with any real cynicism toward religion as such. However, she says that many youth reject the established religious services because of the chasm between what is preached and what is practiced.

Some junior and senior high students become disturbed when their teachers challenge their beliefs. Assigned reading in high school often does the same thing. Church workers may need to give the students guidance to assure them that faith is not so fragile a thing that a teacher or a book can drive it away. Youth must become able to face an opposite viewpoint without fear of being utterly destroyed. The only way such preparation can take place is to face questions honestly and explore them adequately in a church setting.

Strang says that "a person who does not have the courage to doubt may not acquire the wisdom to believe. Part of the antagonism which often occurs at this stage may arise from resentment at having to attend church services in which one no longer finds interest and value." [16] Or, rebellion may stem from the inability to reconcile certain scientific facts with childhood beliefs. The science-theology gap needs bridging. Goldman says that it is the most pressing intellectual problem facing adolescents today if they are to find in Christianity an answer to their search for meaning. When the Bible is taught with a complete disregard for informed biblical scholarship, a whole generation of youth may feel that there are no answers to intellectual problems simply because they have not been exposed to possible solutions. A Youth's faith is not built through avoiding problems.

Adolescent energy drives Youth naturally and normally to question, to discuss and explore ideas for themselves. Using this

energy would make it possible for youth to come to a personal
confrontation with God and with religious truth.

Each individual Youth responds differently to religious doubt.
Some keep up appearances and continue church-going to avoid
open conflict with their parents. One boy said, "I can't stand to
hear mother cry and carry on, so I keep on going to church. I
don't even tell them that I don't believe any more. I just turn
my mind off. I know nothing is going to happen. It hasn't hap-
pened for me in all these sixteen years."

Admittedly, doubt just for the sake of doubt is not constructive. Sometimes, adolescents may try to see *how little* they can
believe and still be called Christians. In the musical *Sure As
You're Born,* one of the characters says, "The truth is I believe
in very little. It wouldn't surprise me at all if I believe less than
you.

> I believe less than you,
> Yes I do, oh I do.
> I believe less than you:
> I can prove that I do." [17]

Adolescents need to be exposed to a structure of religious
beliefs that is strong enough for them to accept or reject. That
is, Youth should be able to respond affirmatively to religious beliefs on the strength of the case as presented—not expected to
believe regardless of how weak the arguments sound.

There are a large number of youth for whom religion is an
intensely meaningful thing. On the whole, it is encouraging that
they are concerned enough to question and to rebel against that
which has no meaning. Dr. Claypool says that the path toward
certainty is always the path of honest doubt. "If you assume the
stance of questioner, the reality will eventually take the shape
of answers. The answers are God's business, and he can be depended upon to give them." [18]

The real tragedy occurs when Youth do not care enough to
question, when they accept wholesale everything that is taught
them, or when they reject the whole package without testing the

contents. Perhaps an even greater tragedy is when the adult leaders ignore the honest questions of Youth or handle them flippantly. This kind of response only leads to further and less wholesome expressions of doubt.

There is, of course, the adolescent who becomes a fanatic. Adult leaders need to recognize this dilemma. If the adolescent becomes deeply caught up in religious life, he may become so split between the instinctual and the spiritual that he rejects his humanity, particularly in its sexual development. He may think that he cannot be religious and please God if he has these feelings. So, he divides himself and denies or rejects his humanity. "A pitfall of the split is that often the adolescent succeeds only for a time in being religious and virtuous. The expelled humanity then returns with devastating power and may shatter to bits the religious superstructure." [19]

As long as fanatically religious individuals can talk about their relationship with God as a private matter, they can avoid confrontation with self. They may even enter a religious vocation to avoid any commitment to God or to people.

The Mysteries of Death and Suffering

"Will you tell me why God let my daddy die? I asked God to make him well, and he let him die. Either God couldn't make him well or he just doesn't care."

Have you ever been asked an unanswerable question?

Goeburg tells of a young Jewish boy who lost his mother when he was twelve years old. He looked at his mother in the coffin and knew that the mother he had loved and the unreal thing in there were not one and the same. Later in life a young married friend of the boy died and left a wife and child. The rabbi said at his funeral that God wanted the young man.

But the boy couldn't buy this explanation. He thought: *How foolish a man the rabbi is! How foolish is anyone in this parlor who believes in what this man is preaching. . . . How can anybody as good as he at 26 years of age, or as good as my mother at 40 years of age, be taken with the excuse that someone by the name of God wanted them more than we here on earth do?* [20]

Adolescents are concerned about death—their own and others. Dr. Knight said he had seen adolescents postpone making vocational commitments because of unconscious fears of death and the feeling that growing up meant growing toward death. It may be that youth are more afraid of life than they are of death.

In the later teens, youth seem to want to find some rational, mature principles to apply to the areas of human suffering and death. They begin to question the whole problem of evil. Some blame God for what to them is the unjust suffering, disease, violence in the natural order as well as in the social order— storms, earthquakes, starving children, etc. "If God is all powerful, why doesn't he stop all of this?" they ask.

We need to realize that most youth come to their teen years with the background of

> Be ye kind
> Jesus loves me
> God can do anything
> God *will* do anything if we only believe
> > if we ask him long enough
> > if we plead hard enough
> > if we give up enough
> > if we crucify self enough.

In the teen years, they begin to think abstractly—they begin to see some of the discrepancies between the rote childhood sayings and the nitty-gritty of realities. And the two do not always stack up in their minds.

Not everyone lives "be ye kind."

They begin to ask:

> *Does* Jesus love me?
> Why does he permit war? Whose side is he on?
> Does he love *everyone?*
> Or, does he just love the good people
> > and punish the bad ones?

Some youth had rather hold on to nursery rhyme religion

than to deal with these apparent discrepancies. One young person admitted that during the Cuban scare, when she was twelve years old, she was so afraid of an attack—of eminent death—that she secretly carried a New Testament around with her. She was ashamed to admit to her parents how afraid she was. She knew she was supposed to "be secure in God's love" and "prepared to die." So, she held on to the New Testament as if it were a charm. This same person, at age seventeen, says she is no longer afraid to die because she is now fully prepared to live.

The Youth worker must walk a fine line when he deals with Youth's concept of God, suffering, and death. He does not want to destroy nor tear down Youth's understanding of God, but to build upon this foundation. He wants to help Youth understand that when he was a child, he thought and spoke like a child. His parents and teachers tried to tell him about God and love in childhood terms, but now he is capable of developing a more adequate concept of God. These books provide help on this subject:

> Your God Is Too Small: J. B. Phillips
> Campus Gods on Trial: Chad Walsh
> God, Pain, and Evil: George A. Buttrick

Somehow, the adolescent must come to accept death as a very natural part of life without blaming God for "taking" a friend or loved one. But the thing that makes it all bearable is that God loves us. God is God when we live. God is God when we die. God always wants the best for man.

Religion and Values

The ultimate in self-realization includes love for something outside and beyond the self. "Ideals and values are not superimposed from without; they develop, to some extent, in response to some need on the part of the individual . . . In a sense, moral and spiritual values are basic to self-esteem, for without hope for the future, it does not matter much what one becomes." [21]

Of course, some youth simply adopt the political, social, and moral values of their parents. They may take the path of least resistance and confine their interest and activities to the status quo. Others, however, use their bodily presence, with noise, signs, and sometimes aggressive actions in protest against the status quo. The student rebellion movements have in the main been confined to the college campuses, but have already begun to move down into the high schools. Churches also are likely to come under increasing attack.

Adolescents are in search of a moral authority. There is a tension between the need to be sure and the need to be free. They want adults to support their moral authority by something more than *mere* authority.

In developing a value system, the adolescent often has a wide gap between what he believes he *should* do—how he thinks he should act or react—and what he actually does. His moral judgment depends not only on the situation, but also *upon the cultural patterns of his sectional society.*

Usdin reminds us that in spite of newspaper publicity, most of the present teens maintain high standards. "These adolescents need and want values to emulate ... They want standards that are definite to rebel against or, if they agree with them, to adopt." [22]

He feels that the new frank rejection of old taboos reflects a mood of regeneration—a determined effort on the part of adolescents to accept a new kind of personal responsibility.

God-relationship does make a difference in the formation of an individual's value system. Dr. Duvall says that "the young person who, deep within himself, feels that he is a child of God is not so easily tempted to act as though human life does not matter ... It is the teen-ager without the benefit of a rich religious heritage who is more vulnerable to the pressures of sheer hedonism, ... partly because he has yet to learn of the values of life in which he may find himself." [23]

So What Does All This Add Up To?

Parents and leaders of Youth sometimes feel completely overwhelmed by the responsibility of prodding young people to develop their own religious beliefs, concepts, and values which have meaning for *their* lives. Adults realize that they often take credit for the success of the well adjusted, acceptable-to-society Youth who has been under their influence but are more reluctant to assume the responsibility for those termed failures.

There is no need to dwell morbidly on failures, but they may help workers re-assess their approaches to leadership. It may be that the attitudes and procedures are basically sound and workers simply have to face the fact that no one person can expect to motivate *every* Youth he tries to lead. On the other hand, some re-evaluation of attitudes and approaches to leadership may be in line. Here are some questions for thought:

1. Have I been expecting Youth to learn *facts* rather than discover *truth?*
2. Have I put too much emphasis on "staying out of trouble," and not enough on doing the right thing for the satisfaction it brings?
3. Have I tried to be the sole source of information in the leader-learner situation, or have I also been a searcher and learner with Youth? "If man and society are to change and grow, the adult world not only has to provide guidance for its youth, but also must be able to hear and profit from the perceptions, indignations, and insights of its youth." [24]
4. Have I been authoritarian in my approach to doctrine and values? Have I given Youth the idea that unless they believe my way, they're dead wrong? Contemporary studies question the conformist character of both society and the church when the whole drive of youth is toward change and finding ways to cope with the new world coming to birth.
5. Have I openly attacked other Christians and Christian groups whose beliefs differ from mine?
6. Have I put such an exclusive emphasis on attendance that I and they consider their presence as a premium paid for services rendered? Have I given them only one choice: To come or not to come? If they come, they're in and I'm successful. If they don't . . . we've both had it! What happens to those who don't come? Do they not still have problems? Do they not still make decisions? choose values? need God?

7. Do I trust the Youth I work with? Youth feel more secure with adults who trust them. They do not feel secure with adults who criticize, condemn, ridicule; nor with those who are always suspicious and jealous. They need to be assured of their worth as individuals.

1. Bob Oldenburg, *Good News* (Nashville: Broadman Press, 1968), pp. 46-49.

2. Dorothy Russell Murphree, *The Mask* (Chicago: The Dramatic Publishing Co., 1967), p. 22.

3. *Ibid.*, p. 23.

4. Ronald Goldman, *Readiness for Religion* (New York: Seabury Press, 1965), p. 26.

5. John Bunyan, *The Pilgrim's Progress* (Philadelphia: The John C. Winston Co., 1933 edition), p. 31.

6. *Op. cit.*, Goldman, p. 164.

7. Robert L. Browning, *Communicating With Junior Highs* (Nashville: Methodist Graded Press, 1968), p. 60.

8. *Op. cit.*, Goldman, p. 22.

9. *Op. cit.*, Browning, p. 23.

10. Charles William Stewart, *Adolescent Religion* (Nashville: Abingdon Press, 1967), p. 68.

11. Robert J. Havinghurst, University of Chicago, *Growing Up in River City* (New York: J. Wilen and Sons, 1962), p. 89.

12. *Ibid.* p. 95.

13. *Op. cit.*, Goldman, p. 12.

14. John Claypoll, "Growing And A Responsive Universe," Crescent Hill Baptist Church, Louisville, Ky., Vol. VI, No. 1, Nov. 10, 1968.

15. Gene Usdin, M.D., editor, *Adolescence: Care and Counseling* (Philadelphia: J. B. Lippincott Co., 1967), p. 34.

16. *Ibid.*, p. 121.

17. Helen Groker and Gene Benton, *Sure As You're Born* (Boston: Baker's Plays, 1967), p. 10.

18. *Op. cit.*, Claypool.

19. *Op. cit.*, Usdin, p. 36.

20. Stephen J. Goeburgh, *The Experience of Adolescence* (Cambridge: Schenkman Publishing Co., 1965), pp. 20-21.

21. *Op. cit.*, Strang, pp. 118-119.

22. *Op. cit.*, Usdin, p. 14.

23. Evelyn M. Duvall, *Today's Teen-Agers* (New York: Association Press, 1966), p. 219.

24. James F. Adams, *Understanding Adolescence* (Boston: Allyn and Bacon, Inc., 1968), p. 228.

Chapter 12. IS THIS ALL?

"IF THE RACE CONTINUES, men will continue to fall in love, to produce children, to work with hand and brain, and to die." [1]

Elton Trueblood wrote in the preface to *The Common Ventures of Life* that his purpose was "to help men and women to prepare for the intelligent and relevant facing of those experiences which are so central to man's life that they have seemed supreme in all generations and cultures. In spite of all changes in the externals of man's life, these go on, though they do not always go on well." [2]

One of the difficulties of communication between adults and youth is that life's common ventures are seen from different perspectives. In December, 1968, Commander Borman of the Apollo 8 space flight was in communication with mission control in Houston, Texas, about the weather. From Houston it was reported that there was "a beautiful moon out there tonight." Borman responded with, "There's a beautiful earth out there." Earthling Lovell, another member of the Apollo 8 crew, observed, "What I keep imagining is that I am a lonely traveler

143

from another planet. What would I think about the earth at this altitude? Whether I think it would be inhabited or not." [3] Perspectives of adolescents, the way they view conditions and evaluate ideas, may seem as different and remote from perspectives of parents and leaders as a view of the moon from the earth compared to a view of the earth from the moon. The problem of perspectives must be taken into account as workers give attention to education and vocation, to preparation for marriage, and to government and society. These life choices are treated separately here because of their importance to youth.

Education and Vocation

All able-bodied, able-minded Youth are faced with the task of becoming economically independent, of making sound educational plans, and of choosing and preparing for vocations.

A group of boys in one very significant survey revealed that their biggest problem was deciding on a career and getting the educational requirements for it. [4]

How well do parents and leaders of Youth understand the flood of decisions which swirl about their heads? Even after decision-making is narrowed to the specific areas of education and vocation, the flood subsides only slightly. For example, Dr. Ruben Roy writes,

> Technology is changing so rapidly that the job of today
> may vanish within a generation or even a decade. [5]

The pressures exerted upon Youth regarding vocation and education are underscored by Strang. She says that "most students must decide in junior high whether they will take a college preparatory course or a commercial or trade school course." [6]

The problems of education and vocation are intensified further by the trend to more dynamic and changing qualities in contrast to the former view of *one* vocation for life. Education is becoming a continuing, life-long process replacing the terminal concept which implied that "when you graduate you're finished!" Such terms as *continuing education, refresher courses, study leave, sabbatical, retraining, upgrading,* and *updating* are familiar already in many vocations and professions. Other terms probably will evolve and crystalize rapidly in the next decade.

The problems inherent in the choice of a vocation are also intensified by the rapid increase in the large number and variety of ways in which persons are earning a living. Some may enter a vocation by way of chance or by following the stream of least demands or by just drifting. One is more likely to find a sense of purpose, usefulness, satisfaction, and success if the best efforts of his mind are brought to bear upon all known factors involved in his choice and practice of a vocation. An understanding of self, aptitudes, and attitudes toward persons and life, coupled with a willingness to explore several possiblities, are helpful processes in the choice of a vocation.

Education is not then an end in itself. Rather, it is the foundation both for earning a living and living a useful, satisfying, productive life.

Here are some guidelines for parents and leaders of Youth as they try to assist their Youth in educational and vocational choices:

1. Try to help each boy or girl gather sufficient information for making a choice.
2. Try to help them make their choices out of healthy motivation; that is, to make their choice for good reasons which they can live with.
3. Avoid pressing for a premature decision.
4. Remember that many decisions will be repeated, altered, perhaps changed several times during one lifetime.

Many conflicts and anxieties are connected with these educational decisions. One seventeen-year-old boy expressed it like this: "To me, the problem of a college education and its aftermath is most depressing. The very idea of the red tape I must go through to get into a college frightens me. At times I feel I am not worthy to go to college . . . I am fearful of what will happen if I go to college and fail. If that were to happen there would be no outlet for me." [7]

Not every youth should go to college! There may be some healthy, capable young people who should not even graduate from a secondary school. Some can receive training commensurate with their abilities and life goals in a vocational, trade, or commercial school. Many Youth, though, are able and probably should complete both secondary school and college. The majority of them should do so, if possible. Adolescents must not be melted into a milky, fluid substance of neutrality and poured into identical, depersonalized molds. They must be helped to become persons . . . persons facing their own educational and vocational choices.

Preparation for Marriage

During adolescent years, young men's thoughts turn to love, courtship, marriage, home, and children. So do young women's! Wouldn't it be tragic if they didn't? Who knows how much these "natural" developments can be attributed to their own body chemistry, or competition of peers, or expectations of adults?

Mothers and father typically experience some anxiety in relation to their offspring during adolescent years as they approach "marriageable age." At some stage, moms and dads are afraid their teen-ager may get married. Later, they are afraid he won't.

Adams advances the theory that some of the concern of adolescents with marriage may not be with marriage as such, but with marriage as a symbol of full adult status. Many teen-agers have grasped for this status which they thought would be assured by marriage.

Youth may be considered prepared for marriage only to the extent that they can openly and honestly face the potential problems of every known area of relationships.

Koonce says about the selection of a mate that "it develops

out of real friendship based upon knowledge of each other, and it grows with time and further acquaintance." [8] He describes four factors involved in genuine love; Respect, Identification, Sexual attraction, and Companionability.

How, then, can workers and parents guarantee that their young people will not make mistakes in their choices of marriage partners and circumstances of their marriages? They can't! But adults will help them discover that love must continue to grow throughout marriage if the husband and wife are to be happy together; and to make this discovery even while each is somewhat motivated by his own dreams and disappointments, convictions and concerns.

In the final analysis, then, each pair of persons must decide for themselves when they are ready for marriage. Efforts at understanding them and their mingled emotions, however, must be reinforced by a worker's own self-understanding if youth are to be supported in their efforts at understanding themselves during one of the most crucial periods in their lives.

Government and Society

"And government of *adults* by *adults* and for *everybody else* shall not perish from the face of the earth!" So lament the youth.

Many young people are unwilling to accept blindly the decisions made by adults which pertain to all of society. Some of them insist upon helping make, shape, and reshape the practices, laws, and codes of ethics. Obviously, all youth are not motivated by the same forces. Many youth are very perceptive, however, and observe along with Foy Valentine that "one of the most persistent heresies in history is the notion that God is chiefly concerned about religion. He is concerned about religion, but he is also concerned about politics and everything else that affects human life. Politics has too long been a lost province for Christians. It is high time to awake to the responsibilities of citizenship which God wills for his people to assume." [9]

Those youth who are struggling with contemporary issues want not sole occupancy in government and civic affairs, but a measure of responsible participation in self-determining processes.

To say that young people do not have necessary knowledge and wisdom for responsible participation is a marked failure to deal realistically with live circumstances. Few youth—if, indeed, any—claim to have all answers to all problems. But they do see many of the problems with remarkable clarity in healthy perspective and are asking fundamental questions. They are aware that "many worthy Christian goals have been sacrificed upon the altars of apathy, ineptitude, and ignorance which Christians have tolerated in the temple of their citizenship." [10]

Youth stand uneasily in the midst of a world of *things* where persons are often reduced to proof-text statistics and multiple excuses for various causes and campaigns. They run head-on into decisions which will not wait, decisions which are shaping their future, decisions for which they are not always prepared. They expel some customary traditional values from central to peripheral areas of their lives while drawing other problems of human need into prominent, central positions for consideration. Neither do they always work on the same problems at the same time or the same priority. Some teen-agers often make bold efforts to correct some of the misdeeds of their elders. They often challenge injustice as they see it, where they see it. They attempt to fix blame at its source. When they think action is needed, they want action—direct action. And they want it now!

Each person is compelled to meet life and make decisions where he finds conditions demanding decision—a task which usually is not easy. The mere attempt at important decisions may produce friction, especially if the youth tries to bring the church and its program under his critical scrutiny. A youth view is portrayed by Samuel D. Proctor in a message to the Baptist Youth World Conference in Switzerland in 1968: "A bewildering phenomenon of today is that the churches of the West have become agents of inactivity, giving sanction to the status quo, blessing the present arrangement, carrying in its membership those who have been unable to negotiate terms with the modern world and who fear change." [11]

Not all young people, obviously, are actively involved in facing the hard questions of life in society. Youth are not all rushing out in wholesale lots to resolve or even deal with the ugly conditions in society. "Never in the history of the United States has there been more interest in participatory democracy but less real participation." [12] There are, however, many notable exceptions, especially among college students. They serve as missionaries, social workers, and some move into political centers to try to bring about change at the *cause* of some problems. High school students, in general, do not have the freedom nor opportunity to invest themselves as fully as college-career youth. They are only a year or two removed from active participation, however.

War, required military service, and the draft are priority matters for many young people, both girls and boys. Some girls experience a general fear of war with nightmares of possible destruction. Some boys resent war or even military service as an intrusion upon their personal plans. Fear doubtless is a factor, too. Both feel that their prospects for advanced education, security in a vocation, and serious thoughts of marriage and home are threatened by military experience. Parents and leaders may make impassioned appeals for loyalty and citizenship values which are unknown or misunderstood by youth. Such appeals can be as unrealistic as passive, purposeless, impersonal participation in military service on the part of a reluctant young person. Churches need to re-think their responsibilities for others at all levels: local, national, and international. Parents and leaders of Youth must learn to listen respectfully when a young person speaks of doubts and even of objections to governmental involvements and prospective military service. Patience and skill are required to help them evaluate their attitudes in making decisions. Each young man should know the options and alternatives to military service by the time he is eighteen.

The president of the National Council for Social Studies has proposed a Youth Corps in which students would serve six to twelve months in community redevelopment, government apprenticeship, and other programs. Such short-term personal involvement would be required within four years after graduation.

Our young people, even as they find opportunity for involvement and action, are not exempt from serious mistakes. However, they are seriously trying to discover and come to grips with the fundamental questions and problems at local, state, national and international levels. They are not ignorant of their surroundings.

With confidence it can be said of youth: They are aware!

So What?

This book—it is hoped—will stimulate adults in so many directions that a few remarks cannot begin to present all of its necessary implications. Perhaps a word is in order, however, about the relationship of adult workers to Youth.

It is imperative that leaders recognize youth as persons, not problems; individuals, not inconoclasts. They are not monsters or some "wholly others" to be feared. They are God-image people trying to make some sense out of their lives. Ruth Strang, (*The Adolescent Views Himself*) suggests that adolescence should be viewed as an *opportunity* and not as a *calamity*.

Maybe those who share relationships with youth could relax and enjoy them more if the idea were relinquished of molding them into perfect, well-adjusted persons—if relationships with them became more give and take. It is rather obvious that no worker has all the answers to all the problems. Workers are learners as well as teachers. "No longer is it merely for the old to teach the young the meaning of life. It is the young who, by their response and actions, tell the old whether life as represented to them has some vital promise, and it is the young who carry in them the power to confirm those who confirm them, to renew and regenerate, to disavow what is rotten, to reform and rebel." [13]

And when they do reject and rebel against what workers say (and they will—they would be nothing more than robots if they did not authenticate what is handed them), the worker should not feel unusually hurt or sensitive about it. How can a youth be helped to become a man if a worker responds to his rejection with childish immaturity?

The following quotation from "What Makes Them Tick?" (From Child Study by Fritz Redl) may prove helpful, even though it was written in the 1940's.

> The reason why we know so little about this phase of development is simple but significant: it is a phase which is especially disappointing for the adult, and especially so for the adult who loves youth and is interested in it. These youngsters are hard to live with even where there is the most ideal child-parent relationship. They are not as much fun to love as when they were younger, for they don't seem to appreciate what they get at all. You can't play the "friendly helper" toward them either—they think you are plain dumb if you try it; nor can you play the role of the proud shaper of youth wax—they stick to your fingers like putty and things become messier and messier the more you try to "shape" that age. Nor can you play the role of the proud and sacerdotal warden of the values of society to be pointed out to eager youth. They think you are plain funny in that role.[14]

1. Elton Trueblood, *The Common Ventures of Life* (New York: Harper and Row Publishers, 1949), p. 9.

2. *Ibid.*, p. 9.

3. *Time*, January 3, 1969, p. 15.

4. Rita Kramer, "The State of the Boy," *New York Times Magazine*, March 30, 1969, p. 97.

5. Gene Usdin, M.D., editor, *Adolescence: Care and Counseling* (Philadelphia: J. B. Lippincott Co., 1967), p. 20.

6. Ruth Strang, *The Adolescent Views Himself* (New York: McGraw-Hill Book Co., Inc., 1957), p. 423.

7. *Ibid.*, p. 427.

8. Ray F. Koonce, *Understanding Your Teen-Agers* (Nashville: Broadman Press, 1965), p. 132.

9. Foy Valentine, *Citizenship for Christians* (Nashville: Broadman Press, 1965), p. 97.

10. *Ibid.*, p. 97.

11. Samuel D. Proctor, "The World of Things," *One World, One Lord, One Witness*, edited by Cyril E. Bryant (Waco: Word Books, 1969), p. 19.

12. "Get Youth Involved in Government, Lower the Voting Age," *Scholastic Teacher*, January 10, 1969, p. 7.

13. W. C. Fields, *Trumpets In Dixie* (Atlanta: Home Mission Board of the Southern Baptist Convention, 1967), p. 49.

CONCLUSION

As YOU READ THIS BOOK you will be living within less than thirty years of the twenty-first century! Children being born now will be expected to live two-thirds of their lives after the year 2000. Our parents and grandparents rolled creakingly into this century on wagon wheels, pulling their past with them. People now are on an aerospace vehicle towed by a terrific vacuum, being sucked at higher and higher acceleration toward the twenty-first century. Patterns of thinking and living now being created or sustained in homes, churches, and schools will come along as basic equipment, or will be left behind as excess baggage as society soars across the next century line!

Writing is a risky business. The authors are continuing to have new experiences, to find more information here and there, to observe pieces of life we have never seen before, and to hear a subdued cry from youth we have never heard before. Therefore, we are constantly faced with the task of reevaluating, rethinking. We intend to question what we have written. We hope you will. This book is by no means an attempt to lay down the law of the Medes and the Persians (nor the Murphrees and the Baptists). As we said in the beginning, we can only hope to prod you to think, to propel you on the endless journey of trying to understand Youth.

We reaffirm our faith in Youth. Despite all the hang-ups and up-tightness of this generation, we believe they are moving toward maturity. Rita Kramer expresses our hope in Youth as she reports the results of a survey made with a group of boys. She said:

> The typical American boy still seems to have more in common with Penrod than with Holden Caulfield or Alexander Portnoy. He is not alienated, not obsessed with sex or revolution, not hung up on pot or protest. His main preoccupation is not girls, his struggle with his parents, or the draft. His world is the world of school and he moves between the gym and the study hall, the cafeteria and the library as concerned with Saturday's basketball game or tomorrow's Spanish exam as his father is with landing a new account or being promoted to general manager.[1]

These are our teen-agers as we see them. We have high hopes for our youth. That's how we *understand youth.*

---

1. Rita Kramer, "The State of the Boy, 1969," *The New York Times Magazine,* March 30, 1969, p. 97.

A WORD TO YOUTH

THIS BOOK IS WRITTEN, by plan and purpose, primarily as a reading-study-resource piece for parents and leaders of youth. We have tried to identify *with* youth rather than merely write about him. You are well qualified to determine whether we have succeeded, and to what extent.

There is nothing in this book which we want to keep from you. In fact, we dare to hope that youth and adults can study this together. We hope you will come closer together, stop talking *about* each other, and begin talking *to* each other—begin to listen to what the other is saying—begin to listen to what the other is.

We dream of improved communications between youth and adults.

Appendix A
Youth and Sexuality

William H. Stephens

The adult does not understand Youth if he does not know something of the frustrations and growing pains Youth have in regard to sex.

This appendix is frank. Every effort has been made to say as tastefully as possible—but without sacrificing communication —what the author feels needs to be said, for if the sexual experience of Youth is ignored, thorough guidance of Youth is impossible.

Some of the ideas of this appendix may be new to many workers (the section on masturbation, primarily). Since some workers have probably not experienced the emotional anguish that accompanies the practice, the section may prove distasteful. The section is included because of the impossibility of understanding the adolescent's sexual development apart from consideration of masturbation.

There are other sections of the appendix which examine the development of sexual attitudes and practices. It is hoped that a thorough study of this material will strengthen the worker's confidence in Christian morality. Attempt has been made to be honest with the available material (as Youth certainly will be). The reader should find that recent research indicates that God had pretty good reasons for the guidelines he gave.

The Biblical View of Sex

"To preach morality is easy. To find a foundation for morality is hard."—Schopenhauer [1]

THE OLD TESTAMENT VIEW

The Old Testament begins with the assertion that all creation is good (Gen. 1 :10,12,18,21,25,31).

Procreation was considered one of the highest blessings afforded man. In fact, the Old Testament laws regulating sexual conduct were largely designed to protect the home and children. This emphasis on procreation is one reason for the toleration of polygamy, possession of concubines, and the levirate law.

A definite progression in attitudes toward sex and marriage is evident throughout Hebrew history. During the period of the patriarchs, wives were considered as property, even though they were the husbands' most prized possessions. (Even so, however, certain laws indicated that polygamy gave rise to evil consequences: Ex. 21 :10–11; Deut. 17 :17; 21 :14.) Prostitution was accepted without serious question so far as a man's conduct was concerned (Gen. 38 :23), but a woman was severely condemned if she had intercourse with her lover (Deut. 22 :21). To become a prostitute was an abomination (Lev. 19 :29; 21 :9; Deut. 23 :18), although Tamar was forgiven because of mitigating circumstances (Gen. 28 :24–26), and Rahab became a heroine because of her conversion (Josh. 6 :25).

Later Old Testament writings reveal a higher view of womanhood. Concurrently, monogamy became the rule and the relationship of one man to one woman became the subject of high praise. Proverbs 31 :10–31 describes the ideal wife in monogamous terms. The various prophets presuppose monogamy.

Thus, progressively, a high view of sex as expressed in a one-man-one-woman relationship seems gradually to have developed through Hebrew history alongside an increasingly better place for womanhood.

Even from the beginning, though, the love of a man and a woman was expressed through sex. There is no record that intercourse ever was only for procreation or limited to biological drives. Abraham's love for Sarah was obviously above a carnal level. The wooing of Rebekah and Isaac's love for her, the love story of Jacob and Rachel, and the story of Ruth and Boaz are indications of deep affection between husbands and wives. Hosea's loyalty to his wife who turned prostitute illustrates a unique perseverance of his love for her.

The sex act, including both sex play and intercourse, is considered normal and good in the Old Testament as an expression of love between husband and wife. Isaac is recorded as "sporting" with Rebekah (Gen. 26:8), an obvious reference to sex play. A newly married man was exempted for one year from serving either as a warrior or in a business capacity which would take him away from home, so he and his bride could enjoy each other (Deut. 24:5). Proverbs 5:18–19 admonishes the man who would be wise to enjoy sex relations with his wife during their youth.

For several centuries, *The Song of Solomon* was considered to be an allegory of the love of God for his people or of the love of Christ for the church. The obvious interpretation, however, is that it is an ode to the love between a man and a woman. The *Song* portrays the fidelity of a young woman who refuses the appealing glamour of a royal court in order to be the wife of a poor shepherd lover. In the story, the full expression of their love for each other comes in the enjoyment of sex and the admiration of each other's bodies.

TWO OPPOSING VIEWS

The Old Testament places sex in healthy perspective. Why, then, has Western civilization come to interpret sex as primarily biological and carnal?

The Western world has a double inheritance: Greek and Hebrew. The Greek view of man was that he consisted of two parts —mortal (evil) and immortal (virtuous). A man's body, with its various drives, made up his mortal nature. The fulfilment of his physical drives was considered to be a necessary evil, even a form of enslavement to passion. His immortal nature was thought to be separate and capable of higher things, but a captive of the mortal body.

The Hebrew-Old Testament view was that man is a unity. Everything about him—body, soul, and spirit, including his background inheritance, physical characteristics, mental prowess, ability, talents, and weaknesses—all combine together to make up his personality (Hebrew word: *nephesh*). The Old Testament view, then, directs God's people *to consider sex as an expression of the total person, not just the biological.*

THE NEW TESTAMENT VIEW

The New Testament is a Hebrew book. It assumes the Hebrew view of the unity of a single personality. Even Paul's discussion of the two warring factions within him (flesh and spirit) is Hebrew-oriented, for *flesh* represents the whole man as evil and *spirit* refers to the whole man in his yearning after good.

Verses such as Ephesians 5 : 22–33; Colossians 3 : 18–19; Hebrews 13 : 4; and 1 Peter 3 : 7 present essentially the same high view of sex as the Old Testament. Husbands and wives should not deny sexual fulfilment to their mates. Indeed, Paul combated the Greek notion that sex is evil by insisting that the marriage bed is undefiled.

The New Testament presents a distinctly higher view of sex than the Old Testament, however. Jesus, when asked about marriage, insisted that men hold to God's original purpose. His reference to *one flesh* was not to the physical union of two bodies, but to the total experience of marriage in which the lives of two persons are blended into one symphony. This perfect blending enables sex to become a full expression of both personalities. Since sexuality involves a person's total personality and makeup, a casual expression of sex becomes impossible, as will be demonstrated later.

Several verses in the New Testament seem to indicate a low view of sex. However, such is not the case. Jesus' reference to eunuchs for the kingdom's sake (Matt. 19 :12) does not indicate a higher level of spirituality for those who remain unmarried and chaste. Rather, he simply points out a focus of life in which a person serves in such a capacity for Christ that would render other attachments difficult.

In the same vein, Paul encouraged men and women not to marry (1 Cor. 7)—not because marriage is a lower state or because sex is bad (see 1 Tim. 3 :2,12; 5 :14; Titus 1 :6; 1 Cor. 9 :5; and other references already noted), but because he believed Christ's return was imminent. In the ensuing world chaos, families could cause a man or woman added difficulty and heartache. Jesus emphasized the same danger in Matthew 24 :19 and Luke 23 :29.

In addition to various teachings regarding marriage, the New Testament explicitly warns against sexual excesses. Adultery, prostitution, and immorality in general are strongly condemned (Matt. 5 :27; 14 :3,4; John 4 :18; 2 Cor. 12 :21; Gal. 5 :19,22; Eph. 5 :3; Col. 3 :5; 1 Thess. 4 :3; to name a few). In fact, several passages (1 Cor. 6 :9–10; Eph. 5 :5; 1 Tim. 1 :10; Rev. 2 :21–22; 21 :8; 22 :15) distinctly teach that sexually immoral persons will be excluded from the kingdom of heaven.

In this context, a Christian should especially consider two things : that sexual expression involves him in all that he is and that the *kingdom* is the full expression of that perfect society which Jesus sought to establish, toward which God is moving mankind, and which exists imperfectly in the hearts of God's people. Since sex not only *expresses* the total personality but also helps *form* it, *sexual conduct becomes a matter of grave importance to the progress of God's kingdom.* Wrong conduct (by biblical standards)—unless corrected by a reorientation of life—renders a person incompetent emotionally, psychologically, and spiritually to relate to other persons in the highest type of society. Conversely, when sex is a part of life under biblical guidelines, it can aid in the full development of personhood which will result in a better society.

THE BIBLICAL VIEW OF SEX APPLIED

"Human beings can 'protect' themselves against venereal disease and pregnancy; they can use pills to avoid physical disaster —but when they do they are dying as persons." [2]

Appeals for premarital chastity have been largely based on the danger of pregnancy or venereal disease. Today's youth (including church youth) are struggling with serious questions regarding sex. The "pill" and other readily-available contraceptives pretty much eliminate the physical dangers of premarital intercourse.

The question, *If we can eliminate the possibility of pregnancy, why should we wait for marriage?* actually assumes a low, unbiblical view of sex. The question which must be explored is rather: *How is sex related to love, personhood, and the development of a better society?*

In reality, if the biblical view of man is correct—that man's nature is unified rather than separate (mortal and immortal)— then sexual relationships (from the simplest touch of the hand in friendship to the ultimate expression in intercourse) profoundly affect a person's entire being. So-called "casual" affairs are impossible. While the relationship of two people who engage in intercourse may be casual, the effects of sexual conduct on the emotions, ideals, personal values, regard for other persons, and one's own self-image are profound. Heavy petting or intercourse outside of marriage inevitably affects a boy or girl adversely and retards his development toward most meaningful personhood.

Marriage is total commitment of one person to another. Sex, at its best, is a total-commitment expression of love. Sex serves as a bonding influence in marriage because it allows for expression of the total person—everything about him, even those subconscious traits of which he himself is not aware. When two people express themselves to each other in such a way, a com-munication of the senses takes place which allows for intimate acquaintance of all the emotions, needs, and expressions of each person with the other. Such acquaintance may create problems between lovers (so-called incompatibility). In such a case, the total commitment relationship within marriage makes possible the reconciling of differences and necessary adjustments so that the two partners can establish conmmon goals and values. (Outside of marriage, sexual incompatibility would likely result in a termination of a relationship which might otherwise have developed into real love if given a chance.) Sex thus becomes not only a bonding influence in marriage, but also contributes to the development of a oneness in marriage which is more pro-found than the sum total of both personalities.

When heavy petting or intercourse is experienced outside of marriage, the fusing of two lives in all of their experiences, moods, needs, goals, interests, and potentials is impossible. Sex becomes primarily a biological release and, while the unmarried partners might experience deep emotions, they miss the most creative potentials of sex. Later, within marriage, emotional and mental patterns will have been set so that the greatest con-tribution of sex to life will be elusive.

The laws of God were given because they aid man in develop-ing to his full potential. Because man is gregarious, he is strongly influenced by society. The relationship of an individual and society is reciprocal. Every person influences society and creates a new society to some degree. On the other hand, society strongly molds individuals. No person can ever be free of the influence of society. Consequently, God's laws are given not only to individuals, but to individuals within the context of living with other people.

Ultimately, the value of every law must be considered in light of what its effects are on individuals and on society in general.

There are views of the psychological and sociological effects of sex which would challenge the view presented here. In the final analysis, then, the source of authority for establishing sexual guidelines must be sought in the Bible with the assumption that God speaks through its pages to guide men to the abundant life. Especially since all of the facts regarding the effects of sexual activity on the total makeup of a person are not yet assembled and evaluated, divine insights into the nature of man and divine guidelines for creating the best possible society are imperative. An ever-increasing body of information indicates that the biblical view of sex is, after all, progressive, creative, and liberating—in the fullest meaning of each word.

Attitude Development

The adolescent years are characterized by tremendous growth spurts, but the rapid growth also takes place in areas other than physical. Spiritual awareness, mental capacity, and personal relationships all make as fast a growth pattern as does the physical.

There are two main goals of adolescence, in regard to sexual development. First, youth must learn to relate in a satisfactory manner to members of the opposite sex. Second, youth must establish and accept his own sex role. This second task refers to the process of a young person accepting what it means to be a man or a woman and accepting and developing the characteristics of his or her sex.

These two goals are, of course, interrelated.

The process should be completed, in most youth, by the age of sixteen. If the tasks have satisfactorily been accomplished, the youth is more pleasant to have around.

.The development of attitudes toward sexual adjustment, as well as the expression of sex, is of very great importance to the youth. Workers and parents will find some answers to their perplexities concerning young people by availing themselves of information regarding this phase of development. Sex, in all of its related influences, is vastly important to the youth himself in the total development and expression of his life. His guilt feelings, his ability to relate to members of the opposite sex, his acceptance of himself as a worthy person, his interpretation of some of the feelings and yearnings he experiences—all of these things and more influence his politeness, rowdiness, communication, surliness, happiness, sadness, school grades, participation in extracurricular activities, attitudes toward adults, and so forth.

For many years, the concept promulgated by Freud—that sex is the dominant influence of life, beginning in the womb of the mother—directed the thinking of those persons interested in adolescent development. Recently, however, modern authorities object to the view (even though they emphasize the importance of the sex drive). The sex drive is, naturally, linked to physical development. And there is a more intensive consciousness of sexual feelings and growth during the adolescent years than before. However, social practices and mores influence the expression of sex and even its development greatly. Desire, privacy, opportunity, and influence of friends all make contributions to the intensity of feelings the Youth has in regard to sex.

A worker with Youth should not make the mistake of thinking that sexual activity begins with puberty. (By sexual activity is meant all of those acts and learning experiences which influence a person's sexual development.) There is no period of childhood in which a person is not developing or learning sexually. In infancy, interest is centered in oneself; in childhood, interest shifts to persons of the same sex; in adolescence, interest shifts to persons of the opposite sex. These "steps" must occur in logical order if a mature sexual adjustment is possible in adulthood. Nor are there abrupt starts and stops with each period; rather, transition periods occur between each period of development and the next.

As the child enters adolescence, it is vital that he learn something of what to expect as a youth. Boys should be prepared for the experience of wet dreams and girls should understand the nature and purpose of menstruation. Otherwise, completely unnecessary and emotionally exhausting guilt, shame, or fear may result. In addition, each sex should know something about the sexual development and attitudes the other sex is experiencing.

The importance of such an education will be pointed up later in this chapter.

During the months the child enters puberty, he may engage in sex play with others of the same age and sex—a characteristic which does *not* indicate homosexual tendencies. In studies, about half of all adults report that they did engage in some form of sex play as children. Likely, there were others who did not report their experiences. This sex play is usually transitory and is soon replaced with normal attitudes toward the opposite sex. The attachment to a person of the same sex is more often attained in simply finding and being a buddy, without any thought of sex play between the two companions.

There are relatively few persons who become sexually active in the true sense before adolescence. Generally, early developers are girls and if they use their newly-developing sex appeal, they do so to gain nonsexual goals rather than for sexual gratification.

Children progress from the chum stage, when they have achieved intimacy of friendship with a single person, to begin moving in a larger group of the same sex. This phase of the relationship of a person to his same sex is important because he learns to relate to a larger society of persons—through being part of a gang or club.

Finally, the age of puberty brings a person to a road—a rather difficult one—which leads to adjustment to persons of the opposite sex. The junior high school years through the twelfth grade (or beyond) are needed for the attainment of this task of growing up. During the transition period from childhood to adolescence, one sex will talk about the other sex, discuss personalities, etc., while not making any overt action toward establishing relationships with a person of the opposite sex. Girls, of course, become interested in boys earlier than the opposite, due to their faster physical and emotional development. They usually demonstrate interest in older boys, for several reasons: The boys of their own age are not responsive to the girls' interests; older boys or men serve as models as girls develop concepts as to what qualities and characteristics they will want in boys; and they are aware (subconsciously) that the older boy or man will not return affection, which relieves the girl of the responsibility of a laison with the opposite sex while allowing her the benefits of affection.

Somewhat the same kind of attachment often occurs with either a girl or a boy to an older person of the same sex—a crush kind of feeling for a person. This kind of attachment can have healthy ramifications because it can fulfil a need of the young adolescent to learn to cope with his upsurging impulses and the older person can serve as a model to imitate. The worker who has felt the affection of the younger youth in such a relationship should handle the case carefully. Forcing an abrupt break in the relationship, showing fright at the circumstance, or encouraging the relationship to fulfil a personal need could result in difficulty in making adjustments in social life later or, in extreme cases, could contribute to an inclination to form homosexual laisons.

Younger Youth are concerned about their maturing process. The shape of their bodies, the size of their muscles, figure development, menstruation, size of sex organs, stature, and masturbation—all are of monumental concern to the young adolescent. Often, when asked about such concerns, they will discuss them as problems of other youth of the same age group. Seldom will they feel free enough to discuss personal problems with sex adjustment and development with an adult. Because they do not know what normal sexual experience is, what others of their own ages really do and think, how pregnancy actually occurs, what is natural and what is unnatural, and what constitutes an evil thought in terms of sex, they experience serious fears and frustrations about natural and normal growth processes.

Boys experience a sharp increase in sexual excitement between the ages of fourteen and eighteen. Their drives make them want to go as far as they can with a girl, while their training places stops on them. The intensity of the sex drive varies with individuals. Those boys and girls who mature early need most help in adjustment because they are biologically equipped to function sexually, but are not prepared to do so emotionally or socially. These youth are those who are most likely to initiate the vulgar conversations about sex and who may experiment erotically with sex. These young persons need guidance, but the guidance must come from qualified persons: either parents or others. Many early maturers, of course, are able to channel their energies into creative outlets and so experience little more difficulty with sexual growth and development than those adolescents who develop at a more normal rate. The late-maturing youth, on the other hand, may have distinct advantages in the long run because of greater intellectual maturity, social experience, and emotional control.

Dating increases during the high school years. During high school, the relationships with the opposite sex become firmly established. A large part of a well-functioning high school is the provision of adequate opportunities for boys and girls to work and play together. Churches, too, normally recognize the importance for such activities. As important as sexual adjustment is in the lives of youth affecting their lives from adolescence on, church Youth activities take on a ministry and educational context.

As a youth progresses in his acceptance of his proper role as a man or a woman, his father influences his decisions greatly. This influence is even greater for the girl. According to studies conducted by Alfred B. Heilbrun, Jr., and others, good relationships with the father are more formative of good adjustment patterns than those with the mother. In fact, several different studies have led to the conclusion that the mother's influence on a daughter is not generally the reason for good adjustment. Other studies have demonstrated that a boy matures with better adjustment when he identifies properly with his father. In addition, Heilbrun found that the characteristics of the mother (feminine or masculine) and those of the father (feminine or masculine) largely determine whether a girl will exhibit femininity or femininity coupled with aggressiveness.

The development of attitudes of girls and boys toward the meaning of sex is vastly different. The worker with Youth should become aware of the characteristics of development of each sex so as to better understand some of the conflicts, dating pressures, and decisions made by youth.

Perhaps the great difference in the sexual development of girls and boys can be capsuled this way : Sex to boys is primarily physical; sex to girls is primarily social.[3] Girls are concerned with the meaning of sex and the development into womanhood relative to marriage: being a wife and mother. Boys are virtually overwhelmed by the new experiences of sex. Masturbation and the boy's attitude toward the practice (molded by his view of life, church teachings, etc.) influence his sexual development perhaps more than any single factor. Masturbation is so important a subject in the understanding of youth that it will be considered in detail later in this chapter.

The hormonal development in boys is much greater than it is in girls. Because of its intensity in the male, the boy is more easily aroused. In contrast, the girl—even though she is biologically as capable of sex as the boy—is prone to relate sex to the establishment of a home, with all of the ramifications of that goal. When a girl responds to the advances of a boy, she responds out of totally different motivations than does the boy.

The boy is more erotic in his sexual interest. The girl is more romantic. The boy has an emotional desire to possess, to feel that he is the master. The girl's sexual desire is primarily in response to feelings of love for the boy. The boy is quite easily aroused sexually; in fact, conversation about sex will arouse him, while the girl may be very objective about the discussion. If a church group conducts a class for Youth in sex education, it should be aware of these characteristics of boys and girls. Workers can assume that a normal boy will be aroused by any discussion about sex, and so should provide some outlet in group activity after the session so as to neutralize his feelings.

The result of the boy's natural tendency to seek to dominate (a tendency which lessens in our society with maturity) and the

girl to be dominated is often that the girl continues her infatua-
tion of a boy even when he "treats her like dirt." The girl who
is weak or insecure has a compounded problem in this area of
relationship because she is prone to identify the boy's rudeness
or brutality as strength. She will put up with his actions because
she feels secure and protected by him.

The tendency for the boy to dominate and for the girl to
allow him to dominate influence all youth, even those who are
not necessarily insecure and weak. The girl is prone to allow the
boy to blow his horn instead of coming to the door, for example.
Parents, concerned that the boy is impolite, should understand
the motivations behind the boy's action and the girl's response
(although they are perfectly in order to insist on polite behavior).

Masturbation

Masturbation was mentioned as being vastly important in
the sexual development of the boy. This subject has been taboo
in past years. Until recently, writers have told of consequences
such as insanity, death, depression, difficulties at school, and
often have given morbid and horror-filled illustrations. Considerable research has been done in recent years, however, by
sociologists, psychologists, and ministerially-trained counselors.

The purpose of this section of the discussion on sex is to provide Youth workers with information regarding the importance
of masturbation to Youth, so they may better cope with the in-
tensities of feelings Youth—particularly boys—have about sex.
The worker, along with church leaders, will make his own judgment as to how to use the information presented here.

Many studies have been conducted since 1915 to determine
the percentage of persons who masturbate during adolescence.
Approximately ninety percent of boys masturbate by early
adolescence. Only a relatively small percentage of girls masturbate and most of them do so infrequently. Studies also indicate
that masturbation is more frequent among the better educated
because of their ability to create satisfying mental images.

Masturbation brings feelings of guilt and worry to boys. Most of them have heard the horror stories told about people who masturbate, and they are incessantly worried because of them. Many feel that they act abnormally. They worry about the thoughts they think in connection with their masturbation.

Because of the easy arousal of the adolescent boy, masturbation is practically inevitable. He feels that he cannot stop, yet generally feels that he should. His desire to quit masturbating, coupled with his overwhelming sexual arousals, bring about constant conflict.

Masturbation seems to be one of the areas of adjustment in which a boy is destined to live alone. After the younger youth years, he will not discuss the matter with his peer group. He does not feel he can discuss it with his parents (even the best-informed parent would have difficulty communicating both the values and dangers of masturbation in a satisfactory manner to his boy) or with anyone else. It is possible, however, that he would discuss the general subject in a group setting with other boys if he could do so without focusing attention on his personal involvement in the practice.

There are some legitimate areas of concern about masturbation. Even though a boy is almost certain to engage in the activity, workers need to be alerted to the dangers and to the values.

On the positive side, masturbation serves to relieve the desire for sex relations and, as such, becomes a release valve to the boy. While this value can be quickly stated and passed over, it should be considered in light of what results would occur if the release valve were not provided. Indeed, some writers, including ministers (such as Charlie Shedd, *The Stork Is Dead*), consider masturbation to be God's provision for good sexual development. Another positive value is that the fantasies associated with masturbation can help a boy adjust to proper relationships with the opposite sex, since he mentally explores ways the girl would react. (However, note the alternate possible effect below.)

Negatively, there are several unhealthy results of masturbation—quite apart from the guilt and anxiety associated with it.

First, masturbation can lead to a view that sex is for personal gratification. This kind of philosophy would reduce womanhood to a plaything level, rather than accepting a woman in the Christian concept that she is a full person. Linked to this danger is another: Masturbation can lead the boy to view the world itself through erotic eyes; that is, he will interpret much of what he sees to have sexual meaning, even when actions, words, or environment is neuter sexually.

Second, masturbation can become a substitute for learning to relate properly to the opposite sex. The practice of masturbation is, at best, an immature sexual expression. The youth who would take refuge in the "safeness" of masturbation without learning to relate (in dating, conversation, mate selection, and so forth) to girls in a mature manner is, in effect, retarding his development and creating difficult marriage adjustment problems for himself. However, such a withdrawal from learning to relate to the opposite sex is an indication of a deeper problem and is not the result of masturbation.

Of course, excessive masturbation could continue even with the boy who does learn to relate well with girls. The danger of excessive practice, however, still exists. The youth will find less meaning in the marriage relationship, since his preoccupation with masturbation indicates a degree of maturity in his relationship with the opposite sex.

The question still exists, *What should a parent, a worker, or a church do in regard to masturbation?* Each person will have to decide the answer to this question on the basis of his background, the quality of instruction the child is receiving, the characteristics of his church, and the openness of both adults and Youth of his area to discussion on the topic. The least that can be said is that Youth should somehow be made aware that masturbation is widely practiced, that the horror stories usually associated with the practice simply are not true, and that the practice does not indicate abnormality. In addition, the Youth should be informed in some way of the dangers of excessive masturbation.

Excessive masturbation sometimes can be traced to a feeling of rejection on the part of the youth by his parents. Consequently, the parent who becomes stern with his boy about masturbation will most likely cause an increase in the activity, rather than a decrease. The youth will interpret the reprimand as further evidence of rejection.

Perhaps information, presented to the youth honestly and without condemnation, will provide the boy with the most help. Full information, given with confidence that the boy will act wisely on it, provides the youth with tools for growth.

The Dating Game

This chapter has attempted to emphasize the close relationship between a youth's adjustment to sexual thought and conduct and his adjustment in all of life's other areas. Dating is the arena where adjustment is primarily carried out. As a youth dates, he will accept certain characteristics of his mate and reject others. Gradually, the boy and the girl will form opinions which eventually coalesce (ideally) into the kind of husband or wife each wants. By the very nature of the dating experience, many crises will arise, along with the happy experiences. A girl will learn how to please a boy while maintaining (and developing) her moral views, and what kind of boy she wants to please. She will learn to recognize romantic overtures as sincere or conniving. During the learning process, she will live through many heartaches. A boy will also learn what characteristics to accept and reject in a girl, and which girls he considers to be worth his dating effort. Both sexes all the while will be learning how to relate to the opposite sex.

In considering attitudes toward sex, the worker with Youth also needs to evaluate—and help Youth evaluate—healthy attitudes toward dating. In contemporary society, sex attitudes and practice are inseparable from dating. Dating practice sets conditions which influence the degree of sexual experimentation and influence the boy and girl in setting limits on petting.

Two extremes are possible in the parent's attitude toward his boy or girl dating. Some parents may feel that with dating sex is a constant danger (by sex, they would mean heavy petting or actual relations). The other extreme is seen in those parents who rush their youngsters into dating early. The decision as to when a boy or girl is old enough to date is more logically made when the total process of mate selection is considered. As has been noted earlier, a youth establishes peer group relationships prior to opposite sex relationships. When he has established satisfactory relationships with his own sex—and only then—he is ready emotionally and developmentally to do so with the opposite sex. He begins by relating to the opposite sex in groups. He group dates. He "pairs off" and "meets someone at the party," but he is not yet ready to seriously relate to a girl individually. Gradually, he learns to relate to girls individually, until full dating takes place. Girls must go through the same kind of procedure, even though they are not normally the aggressors in the dating relationship and even though they mature earlier.

During the dating years, the boy and the girl must be about the business of determining the kind of mate each wants to spend a life with. This process of selection is, needless to say, tremendously important.

If a youth is forced into the dating relationship too early, he is made to skip over a vital learning procedure: relating to his own peer group. A boy or girl cannot establish mature, healthy relationships with the opposite sex without learning to relate to his or her own sex. On the other hand, if a girl or boy is required to wait until the age of fifteen or sixteen, without any consideration of the importance of group dating in adolescent development, a parent runs the dangerous risk of not allowing the youth to gradually learn to relate to the opposite sex. The girl, for example, is thus forced into a dating relationship with a boy who has had two, three, or four years of experience in learning to relate to girls. She is emotionally unprepared for the experience. Rather than protecting their daughter, parents who force a girl to skip much of the vital learning experience actually cause her to face life experiences for which she is woefully unprepared.

A balance needs to be maintained between over-indulgence and strictness. The guidelines need to be based *on the way God created people to develop* in their relationships with other people. Although parents may have many an anxious hour when they would prefer to have their youth at home, a step-by-step experience in mate selection provides a good foundation for a happy marriage.

Going steady is a matter of grave concern to parents and youth workers, and the experience of steady dating with one person is related to the overall learning experience of youth. The value of going steady is in the youth's learning to relate to the opposite sex during many different moods over a period of time. Youth point out reasons such as: always being guaranteed a date; able to relax better; not having to worry so much about what is worn and not having to plan so far ahead.

Some pitfalls of steady dating are: a youth does not learn to relate to enough different people. Therefore, the process of mate selection seriously suffers. A youth increasingly faces the possibility of sexual intimacy, due to being with one person frequently. A youth is not necessarily on his best behavior, thus he does not develop his own personality as much as he could. A youth tends to focus attention on things he and his steady like as a couple. Consequently, he eliminates himself from many new and interesting experiences which could give new clues to his potential.

The experiences young people have with love are intense and absorbing. The feelings in young love are more overwhelming than mature love. These experiences are necessary, however, for the youth to grow up prepared for mature love.

The boy faces a particular danger, in that his sexual impulses are more erotic, of bringing into *one person* his views of sex and his views of the ideal girl. If he learns to date one kind of girl to fulfil his sex urges and another kind of girl whom he would consider of potential worth as a wife, he treads on the very dangerous ground of poor sex adjustment. His married sex life will most likely be unsatisfactory and the possibilities of promiscuity after marriage are much greater.

Understanding Opposites

It is of very great importance that youth of both sexes learn the particular characteristics of the other sex. Misunderstandings can lead to serious conflicts while dating, since an action or word might mean something entirely different to one sex than to the other.

Boys generally feel proud of sexual conquests and often boast of their exploits to their peers. Although this characteristic would not be as true among church-oriented boys, the boy rarely faces the degree of shame girls face for similar conduct. Girls (except in rare circumstances) lose self-respect if they engage in sex exploits and their actions become known. A girl should be aware of the importance a boy's peer group attaches to sex relations, so that she will not allow herself to be used to satisfy the boy's desire for peer acceptance. The boy should be aware of the girl's certain loss of self-respect and peer respect, so that he will not be so apt to disregard her future.

A key problem in sex adjustment for boys and girls is that each sex does not generally understand how sexual feelings occur and develop with the opposite sex, nor what meanings are attached. Such knowledge would further serve as guidelines for youth to follow as they face explosive situations.

A boy may feel that a girl has the same kind of erotic urges that he has. Girls may not, on the other hand, be aware of the compulsive nature of sex to a boy. Since feminine nudity excites a boy, he naturally thinks that a girl is as excitable. The girl, since male nudity does not excite her and is in most cases repulsive, cannot know by instinct that certain actions on her part

will be interpreted by the boy as sexual gestures. Unintention-
ally girls may act quite innocently in such a way to arouse a boy.
The boy, however, does not realize that the girl is acting innocently. Physical contact, completely innocent, may excite a boy.
Conversation about sex, engaged in innocently by the girl, will
be erotic to a boy.

To be sure, a girl often dresses in order to be sexually appealing, but even when she does, she usually does not realize the potential consequences of arousing a boy sexually. Certainly she
cannot understand, at adolescence, the force of a boy's sexual
feelings.

The importance of understanding the meaning of sex to the
opposite sex is heightened intensively when single dating begins. A girl's desire to be loved can be satisfied on many levels of
physical contact. A kiss and an embrace can be healthy both to
the older boy and the older girl who have learned to handle their
emotions on such a level. The same experience, however, can
strongly arouse a younger adolescent boy. When petting pro-
ceeds beyond the kiss and simple embrace, however, the girl
probably does not realize how explosive a situation she is letting
herself in for. Even the practice of caressing a girl's shoulders
approaches the limits of a normal boy's ability to control his
actions. Unless he cares for the girl enough to be concerned
about her future, he will most probably go as far as the girl will
allow him to go from this point. The kind of snuggling and
caressing which usually takes place in a parked car or in an
unchaperoned home setting can be enjoyed by the girl for expressions of love, since these actions hold romantic significance
for her. She believes that the boy receives the same kind of
pleasure, when in reality petting is an emotional prelude to him
for intercourse.

Certainly, the training which a youth receives makes a great
deal of difference in the meaning attached to such preliminary
stages of love-making. In the first place, the more mature male
youth would not be likely to park with a girl he cared nothing

about. When he parks with a girl toward whom he has romantic notions, he is prone to be more concerned about her future, and so by past experience he has set some boundaries of his own. The mature Christian boy and girl are reasonably well prepared to cope with their sexual impulses. Nevertheless, they are human. If they care deeply about each other, they are prone to become more intimate with each other, even if they have both drawn the line short of actual intercourse.

With the youth who is not so mature, of course, the dangers of parking are more profound.

Physical yearnings for sexual expression normally do not come into play with the girl until considerable arousal has already taken place. Under such circumstances, the girl, unless she has by past experience become interested in the act of sex to fulfil immature or abnormal needs, will already have become satisfied that the boy has somewhat the same romantic attachments to the sex play that she has.

The girl who naïvely assumes that the kissing and caresses mean the same kind of enjoyment to the boy as to her suddenly finds that the boy has become aroused to the point where his advances are difficult to control. The boy, on the other hand, may be dismayed and angry at the girl for actions which he interpreted as "leading him on." The girl, in such cases, is at fault for not taking into account the kind of sexual drive the boy has to contend with. The boy is at fault for not understanding the nonerotic nature of the girl's willingness to park and enjoy a certain amount of love-making.

When a girl gives in to a boy's advances, she generally does so out of love for him. Girls who feel unloved at home because of lack of parental attention or other demonstration of the parents' love may become promiscuous in their sex lives as part of a search for acceptance by a man. The average girl who lets a boy have intercourse with her does so, though, because she feels that he really loves her. She engages in the act to please him. This is not to say that the girl does not enjoy the sex act. It is to say,

rather, that her enjoyment is not primarily erotic. She interprets the sex act in terms of a home, marriage, and children,
even though such events may be in the future.

A major difficulty the girl has is being honest with herself
regarding the boy's intentions and love. A boy who has not ma-
tured in his attitudes toward sex has learned early the importance of convincing a girl that he loves her. If the girl is roman-
tically attracted to the boy, she is prone to follow her emotions
and believe the boy, even though she has the nagging feeling
that the boy is not really on the level with her.

Curiously, the boy is more apt to attempt intercourse with the
girl early in their relationship, while the girl is more apt to refuse. As the boy develops a sincere attachment to the girl and
becomes more interested in her as a person, he becomes more
reluctant to subject her to the possible results of intercourse—
pregnancy, loss of self-respect, loss of peer approval, agony of
parents, loss of educational opportunities, and the other possible consequences of the sex act. The girl, on the other hand,
more certain of the value and strength of the relationship, may
be more willing to engage in sex play, even intercourse.

These paradoxical characteristics serve as a check and balance system in mate selection and moral purity, up to a point.
There may come a point, however, when the young couple have
such intense feelings for each other that they no longer have the
strength to call a halt to love-making before it goes too far.
Petting progresses nearer intercourse each time a couple engages in love-making. With each succeeding parking experience, emotions are aroused more quickly and the limits on love-
making shift more toward the danger point. There seems, then,
to be a cumulative effect in petting. "Going all the way" is most
likely to occur not as a preplanned act, but when the emotional
chemistry of both the boy and the girl is at its most explosive
point. In such a case, the couple would not likely be prepared
with a contraceptive. The danger of pregnancy, then, is compounded. If the youth are strongly oriented to Christian moral

values, they likely would resolve not to make the same mistake again. However, after achieving the intimacy of intercourse once, and experiencing such strong feelings of love for each other, it is unlikely that they would be strong enough to overcome the urge to engage again in the sex act. Again, though, due to the strength of the Christian couple's convictions and their prior resolve not to engage in sexual relations, they would not likely be prepared with contraceptives, this time, either. The worker should be aware of and should alert Youth to such an explosive situation so that Youth will recognize the need for maintaining high sexual morals.

The worker should be aware that Christian Youth have the same intensity of feelings sexually and toward mate selection that other youth have. To be sure, Christian Youth have moral strengths that the average youth does not have, but once the chemistry of emotions which lead to intercourse are unleased, the church Youth is in a potentially tragic circumstance, due to his and her desire to not "let it happen again."

Incidentally, Kinsey's studies revealed that the girl's home was most often the place where premarital intercourse took place. The boy's home and the automobile were the second and third most likely places. He conducted his research in 1953, and the availability of the automobile may have changed the order since then, but at least his studies point up the importance of proper chaperoning in the home.

Social Acceptance of Sex

Both adults and youth are concerned about socially-acceptable attitudes and practices toward sex. Attitudes are, of course, as diversified as the social strata of society. Between puritanism and pornography there exists a wide divergence of opinions. Many competent authorities in the past have insisted that premarital sexual relations guard against future psychoses and aid a person in emotional and interpersonal adjustments. Strang points out [4] studies by Margaret Mead which compared girls in the Manus tribe who practice complete sexual repression and Arapesh adolescents who can choose between chastity and sexual indulgence. Compared to the Samoans, who are unrestricted in their childhood sexual activities, she found that the adolescents in those tribes which repressed sexual desires during youth experience no more stress and strain in growing up than those who do not repress their sexual impulses. College students are often told that sexual repression brings about frustration, but this view is not supported by research.

Many factors determine a youth's attitude toward sex. How early dating starts, the happiness of home life, the amount and kind of sex education, and other physical and emotional factors enter into the formation of an attitude.

Religious orientation is a large factor in attitude. Evidently, the devoutness of one's religious orientation is of more importance than denominational affiliation.[5]

Obviously, the conflicts of what society *demands* from youth in sexual expression and what it *promotes* cause anxiety among youth. Their yearning for social acceptance, which generally includes abstinance of sex relations prior to marriage, is confounded by sex-heavy advertisements, movies and drama which exploit sex, and the appeal of the sexual experience as promoted through various media. In addition to these obvious conflicts, society provides very little guidance to the youth in his search for sound sexual adjustment. Lack of information regarding sex is caused by a timidity about the subject. The result is that youth often are left to sail the sea of sexual education alone. Often, when information is given, it is negative—emphasizing the danger of pregnancy and sometimes distorting the facts. Such an approach indicates to the youth that if he can avoid the dangers described by adults, the sex act is all right. Studies have indicated that youth have given positive reasons as why they avoid premarital intercourse—religious instruction, family teachings, and desire to wait until marriage—more often than negative reasons.[6]

The general attitude of boys to the sex relationship have been discussed. It would be beneficial, however, to consider further the effect of sexual promiscuity on the adolescent.

The boy, as has been noted, is not looked upon derogatorily by his peer group (except in a church group, and then not always seriously). The boy is considered to have made a conquest. The girl, however, must face up to her ego and self-esteem as a person who has *been* conquered. She knows that she has been used by the boy. Considering sex as a prelude to romance as a girl naturally does, she can't understand why a boy would make her "do such a thing, and then drop me." There is often a feeling of guilt, a feeling which sociologists consider to be more widespread than reports indicate, due to the fact that many girls would not truthfully admit guilt because of their shame (subconscious). A girl may develop feelings of hostility toward the boy who engages in the sex act with her. Having submitted to his advances because of feelings of love, she comes to realize that she is "only a body to him." Of course, if the relationship deepens in love and the couple become engaged, and later marry, this characteristic may not apply. The girl possibly will, in such a case, be satisfied that she was engaging in a real expression of love. The danger in such a premarital relationship lies in the fact that engagements are often broken and do not develop into marriage.

In short, then, good moral attitudes and practices are important to the girl not only because of averting the danger of pregnancy, with all of the attendant problems, but also because of the girl's mental health. Her self-esteem, self-respect, and the development of her own self-image are seriously affected when she engages in the sex act in a way different from her training. These results are important from a psychological viewpoint, even if religious reasons are not considered. Of course, Christian values are based on insights which God has about human nature. He provided guidelines for conduct which he knew would provide the greatest possible happiness for persons.

The boy also has implications to consider. Thomas F. Staton [7] points out that "one cannot exploit others—deliberately subject others to injury and danger—without injury to one's own integrity and mental health." He further describes the effects of a boy's promiscuity as developing attitudes of exploitation, self-centeredness, and disregard for the welfare and happiness of members of the opposite sex. Such attitudes will seriously affect the boy's own chances for marital happiness, and such attitudes will also affect the boy's future relationship with other persons. Staton writes, "I believe, from twenty-five years of clinical experience, that the effects of sexual promiscuity on boys' and girls' personalities, and on their prospects of good mental health and marital adjustment, constitute more than adequate grounds for making continence prior to the marriage relationship a valid and desirable objective of sex education."

The boy who is aware of such certain results of his seducing a girl is more apt to consider his actions. Certainly, he will not plan to seduce a girl he really cares about. Awareness of the reasons for a girl's response to sex, too, will give a boy solid reasons for Christian morals. The boy who seeks to prove that he is sexually irresistible to girls is simply uninformed as to the reasons for a girl's response to sex.

As the worker considers the importance of sex and dating to the Youth with whom he works, he needs to think through each response of a Youth to the long-range results. No act is exclusive. Every act of a youth has implications about attitude and future development.

Additionally, parents and workers need to seriously examine the value of a program to teach Youth about sex—not just the biological aspects, but what sex means in the totality of life; what it means to be a boy or girl; what the opposite sex expects out of a dating relationship; what sexual motivations the opposite sex experiences; what makes each sex respond to a kiss and an embrace; what are danger points in petting; what effects premarital intimacy have on a person's life and future marriage; what values chastity and positive morality have on a person's life and future marriage.

Since the youth cannot be considered apart from his sexual

development, a parent and worker need to consider answering the needs—sometimes crying-out-desperately needs of Youth.

1. Quoted by Douglas Rhymus, *No New Morality* (Indianapolis: The Bobbs-Merrill Company, Inc., 1964), p. 11.
2. Peter A. Bertocci, *Sex, Love, and the Person* (New York: Sheed and Ward, 1967), p. 111.
3. William Simon and John Gagnon, "Psychosexual Devopment," *Trans-Action*, March, 1969, p. 13.
4. Ruth Strang, *The Adolescent Views Himself* (New York: McGraw-Hill Book Co., Inc., 1957), p. 329.
5. Evelyn M. Duvall and Sylvanus M. Duvall, editors, *Sex Ways in Fact and Faith* (New York: Association Press, 1961), p. 116.
6. *Ibid.*, p. 117.
7. James F. Adams, editor, *Understanding Adolescence* (Boston: Allyn and Bacon, Inc., 1968), pp. 255-256.

Other Sources

Alfred B. Heilbrun, Jr., "Sex-Role Identity in Adolescent Females: A Theoretical Paradox," *Adolescene*, Vol. III, No. 9, Spring, 1968.

Ira J. Gordon, "The Continuing Search for Identity," *Human Development: From Birth Through Adolescence* (New York: Harper and Brothers, Publishers, 1962).

Gene L. Usdin, M.D., editor, *Adolescence: Care and Counseling* (Philadelphia: J. B. Lippincott Co., 1967).

John C. Howell, *Teaching About Sex* (Nashville: Broadman Press, 1966), p. 76.

Appendix B

Evaluation of Survey of Southern Baptist Youth

by Merton Strommen

How the Survey Was Conducted

During the winter of 1968-69, the Sunday School Department and the Research and Statistics Department of the Sunday School Board of the Southern Baptist Convention began a research project to determine some characteristics and views of Southern Baptist Youth. The survey is not yet completed. The information included in this appendix is weighted in favor of the above average youth, the female sex, and the years thirteen-fourteen. This information is presented with the possibility that further research may call for adjustments in the findings. All youth originally selected did not respond, even in follow-up efforts. Sixty-three percent of the first two groups responded; 80 percent of the third group; and 78 percent of the fourth group. The average response was, therefore, 72 percent. Obviously, those youth who did not respond were in most cases the least active. Consequently, the reader will draw the conclusion that the survey is biased toward the faithful and nominal Southern Baptist Youth. The findings cannot be considered representative of the *average* Southern Baptist Youth, then, but rather of the slightly *above average* youth, in terms of their active participation in the church.

There were 317 participants in the survey who could be designated as less active, 732 more active. Forty churches were in the open country, 353 were of other types, such as city or suburb. There were 460 boys and 589 girls surveyed in the following high school grades: freshmen—309, sophomore—289, junior—209, senior—148, graduates—27. In addition, adults who work with youth were tested. They were instructed to respond to some questions according to their own viewpoints, but to others according to their concepts on how the youth were responding. This procedure was designed to measure the margin of the communication gap.

In addition to those surveyed at random, another survey, using the same materials and directives, was conducted at Glorieta and Ridgecrest during the summer of 1968. One thousand and thirty-three youth were surveyed. The results were kept separate from the random survey, for later comparison. The results, as will be noted, were significantly different.

Strengths Revealed by the Survey

There are three major strengths which emerge from the data: religious earnestness, high evaluation of church youth groups, and aspirations to a life of service.

RELIGIOUS EARNESTNESS

Significantly, the Youth involved in the study reflect strongly positive attitudes toward their churches and keen interest in guidance, especially that which relates to the deepening of personal faith. This attitude of interest and eagerness is a pervasive one which shows little variation when comparisons are made on the basis of region, size of community, size of church, sex, etc. Even less active Youth who normally tend to be negative toward their congregations show positive attitudes which rank above those which typify Youth of other denominations.

This positive attitude is coupled with a religious earnestness. When, for instance, church attendance, Bible reading, incident of prayer, and percentage of giving were used as criteria for religious activity, the Southern Baptist Youth in a survey sample ranked well above the other denomination youth groups.

Basic to this religious earnestness reflected by the Southern Baptist Youth is their sense of identification with the Christian faith. Fewer than usual are troubled by an uncertain relationship with God. A high proportion believe they are loved and forgiven by God, a relationship which they cherish.

YOUTH GROUP

The second major area of strength is reflected in the evaluation which the sample Youth gave of their church Youth groups. In evaluating the general spirit and *esprit de corps* of their groups, they rated them higher than did the youth of other denominational groups.

Interestingly, the highest evaluations of group spirit are given by those in the largest congregations (over 1,000 members) and by village youth (less than 2,500 inhabitants) of the southeast region.

Comparatively speaking, the attitudes of Southern Baptist Youth toward their church Youth groups must be regarded as a strength and an important element in the future planning.

ASPIRATIONS FOR SERVICE

A majority of the Youth aspire to a life of unselfish service to man and sincerely desired to accomplish God's will for their lives. Two out of three declare their interest in some form of service to man; one out of two see this service in terms of removing social injustice; and two out of five declare "much interest" in some church-related vocation.

Where is one more likely to find this mission orientation, this desire to be caught in the life of meaningful service? The answer seems to be this: in the large congregations. No variations of any significance appear between region, size of community, sex or year in school.

There is one obvious implication that should be noted at this juncture in the report. Special note needs to be made of the fact that the Youth of the church do represent a separate subculture whose aspirations, loyalties, and commitments stand in sharp contrast to the most highly publicized subcultures. They are willing and desirous of assuming significant responsibilities in tasks which are in line with the mission of the church and with the crucial issues of our day. Their sense of mission goes beyond perpetuating institutional loyalties and fellowship to a reaching out as a potent force in today's society.

Most Troublesome Concerns

One fourth to one third of Southern Baptist Youth are much worried or bothered over such matters as: lack of family unity, strong dating emotions, questions about life partner, lack of self-confidence, acceptance by classmates, personal problems, and the faults of adults. These proportions are significantly higher than those found for Youth in three other national populations. It may be that these concerns tend to be found in the south or in the regions which are especially strong for Southern Baptist churches. But to isolate the causative factors and determine why these concerns are more widespread in the Southern Baptist congregations is the complex issue that is beyond the scope of this study. What is more important now is the fact that a significant proportion of the Youth are troubled in these areas and look to *their churches for help.*

Significantly, these expressions of concern do vary by such variables as region, size of church, size of community, and year in school.

Variations by Subgroups

The most troubled of the Youth are those who are in the ninth grade, freshmen in high school, and the least troubled are the seniors. Each successive year in school, the concerns are less.

Greater concern is expressed by Youth of the southeast states who live in small towns (less than 2,500 inhabitants). They report more distress over a lack of family unity, lack of personal assurance, and greater feelings of personal guilt. When the

Youth in cities of inhabitants of 10,000 or more are compared by region (southeast versus southwest), the differences noted above disappear.

If there is a surprise, then it comes when dividing the Youth by size of congregation. For reasons not yet apparent, the size of the congregational fellowship is a significant variable that shows its impact in the degree to which their Youth are troubled over emotional issues. Without question, the advantage is found with congregations of memberships from 500 to 999. When their Youth are compared to those in the smallest congregations (under 200 members) we find them significantly less bothered over: lack of family unity, parental misunderstanding, strong dating emotions, personal assurance, academic problems, relation to teachers, and personal problems. Somehow there is an ameliorating influence in the fellowship which is generated in congregations whose membership is between 500 and 1,000.

Specified Concerns

At this point, it may be helpful to pinpoint the kind of concerns that are especially troublesome to freshmen and sophomores of small congregations in smaller communities.

Whenever adults are mentioned—parents, teachers, or congregational leaders—greater concern is expressed. Without question, a significant percentage of Southern Baptist Youth are troubled by their relationships with adults and feel that there is a lack of communication, proper respect and consideration accorded them as Youth.

A second major theme which recurs in the items relates to anxiety. The Youth show themselves to be anxious and worried about many matters—self-criticism, self-blame, feelings of inadequacy, and lack of confidence. Concerns such as these can be debilitating to young people, especially if they are bottled up out of a fear that "if I were a good Christian I would not feel this way." There is a task of healing tender spirits lest they carry emotional scars into adulthood. Many of these personal issues would change rapidly if shared with the concerned adult as in counseling or in a small group where there is freedom to share innermost thoughts and feelings.

A third major theme revolves around a deep desire for a more profound experience of God, a dissatisfaction over their present Bible knowledge and a feeling of distance from Christ. This kind of concern is associated with religious earnestness and bespeaks a hunger that notes a healthy conflict.

A fourth theme, and an intense one, is the emotional response of worry, concern, and often fear that is associated with thoughts of a life partner.

The subculture within which Southern Baptist Youth live and learn has generated concern which cannot be ignored. The question is not whether these concerns are good or bad, or whether they reflect on a church or not. The question rather is this: *How can Youth ministries move in ways that will help the Youth face these personal issues in a healing way?*

Beliefs

It is evident that many tend to identify external behavior with the Christian faith. Hence, doing what is generally disapproved by the congregation is seen as committing a sin. Many believe that they are outside of grace until they repent of the infraction and are forgiven.

The tragic effects of an overstress on external behavior is to trivialize the profound and sinister power of sin and by implication trivialize the power of grace, of trusting in his promises and his continuous presence.

Another tragic effect of stressing standards is to increase the fear of being judged. As a result, Youth find it difficult to admit to their struggles and sins. They are encouraged, rather, to act and talk as those who live up to the standards which are presented as marks of the dedicated Christian life.

This issue, a subtle and disturbing one, relates to the word *pretense*. One of the important conclusions of the Lutheran study was that the youth tend to enter the doors of their churches and leave their deepest concerns and human struggles outside the door. Later, when leaving the meeting, they again shoulder the concerns that have remained hidden and move on, not having related them to the Christian faith or the healing experiences of sharing them in a group. This problem seems also to characterize the church Youth groups of the Southern Baptist congregations. Though the Youth are usually friends and enjoy being together, they admit that they are not at ease in sharing their personal problems and declaring their innermost thoughts.

This next issue is a common one. Namely, youth's perception of the particularity of Christian faith. It is an issue that is not unique to any one denomination because church people everywhere are giving assent to a generalized religion and assuming it to be Christianity.

Though most (87 percent) see Jesus as the Divine Son of God, believe in the Trinity (81 percent), miracles (88 percent), and the hereafter of heaven and hell (91 percent), upwards to half agreed to religious statements which made Christ unnecessary. "Being sincere in whatever you believe," and "trying sincerely to live a good life" is deemed adequate for about two in three as a way to peace with God. Human effort (sincerely trying) instead of divine intervention (being saved), is part of the everyday theology of Baptist Youth. This is evident also in their concept of grace (conditional) and their concept of sin (external acts). There is a need for meetings that engage the Youth in thinking through their stereotypes of the faith as they relate to Scriptures.

Variation by Subgroups

There are regional differences between the Youth of the southeast and those of the southwest. Youth in small towns (less than 2,500 inhabitants) report less family unity, greater uncertainity over their relationships to God, and greater feelings of personal guilt. They are less humane in their attitudes and more in doubt as to what they believe. On the positive side, village Youth of the southeast region give higher evaluations of their Youth groups and show a greater eagerness for help from their churches. These differences vanish, however, when the city Youth (over 10,000) of the two regions are compared. The only difference of significance is the greater religious activity, and less problems with morals among city Youth of the southeast.

Size of congregation is one of the most significant variables. Youth in the smallest congregations are the most troubled over: lack of family unity, parental misunderstanding, strong dating emotions, personal assurance, academic problems, relationship with teachers, and personal problems (guilt). Youth in churches size 500 to 999 are significantly less troubled by these emotional issues. Likewise, their Youth are more religiously active, more humane in their attitudes, and believe more of what their church teaches. The one area where size of church is not a factor is quality of Youth group participation and spirit, and desire for guidance from the church.

Another significant variable is age or year in school. The most troubled Youths are the ninth graders. Each successive year the concerns are less. This consistent phenomenon did not appear in the other denominational studies.

Remarkably, there is no change in increased or expressed values during the four years. But increments of gain are seen in scores which assess human relations, justification, Christian concepts, and certainty of belief. There is an encouraging growth in perception and sensitivity by year in school.

What the Survey Revealed

SOCIOLOGICAL INFORMATION

One difference between those Youth surveyed at the assemblies and the random survey was occupation of parents. Assembly Youths had a much higher percentage of parents who were in professions such as medicine, law, teaching, ministry—a difference likely due to the fact that many Youth whose parents are in full-time religious vocations attend assemblies.

Other differences which are significant are:

1. Assembly Youth revealed fewer problems with the family illness than random survey Youth.
2. Difficulties in the home due to financial problems occur more often with random survey Youth.
3. Many more assembly Youth have parents who are high school and college graduates.
4. More assembly Youth report that both parents are members of the same church.
5. Many more families of assembly Youth have family devotions regularly in their homes.
6. A significantly higher number of assembly Youth reveal the desire to become ministers or missionaries, while about the same percentage of each group (assembly and survey) showed interest in becoming social workers.
7. The assembly Youth were far more active in Youth activities at their local churches than the Youth surveyed at random.

The surprising fact revealed by the survey was the affluence of Southern Baptist Youth. They have a considerable amount of spending money. This affluence makes it possible for Southern Baptist Youth to participate fully in the youth subculture.

OTHER INTERESTING FACTS

A very high percentage of Southern Baptist Youth never drink alcoholic beverages.

About half of the mothers of Southern Baptist Youth are employed one half to full time outside the home.

Almost one third of Southern Baptist Youth—of both assembly and random samplings—have trouble getting along with their parents.

Eighty-four percent of the random sampling and 90 percent of the assembly sampling attend church more than half of the time.

COMPARISON BETWEEN BOYS AND GIRLS

In the general areas of frankness, concerns, interests, church teaching, and attitudes, the differences between boys and girls were not widely divergent. However, some differences were revealed.

Boys have somewhat more problems with parental understanding than do girls, more problems with dating and controlling their emotions, more problems with personal morals, and less personal assurance. Boys revealed a greater interest in adventure-related goals in life; girls, a greater interest in religious activities. Girls were more concerned about church teachings on human relations.

A surprising concern was revealed by all Youth on their certainty of belief. The assembly Youth were only slightly more certain of their beliefs than the random sampling. This characteristic is revealed in various ways throughout the survey.

RELIGIOUS PRACTICES AND ATTITUDES

One of the brightest spots in the survey was the characteristic of loyalty to the church with Youth consistently revealed. Almost half of the random sampling indicated habits of giving eight percent or more of their income to church or charity; 89 percent indicated church attendance one or more times per week; 37 percent claimed to read the Bible several times per week, and another 34 percent about once a week; a very large majority indicated that prayer was a regular practice.

Almost all Southern Baptist Youth believe in God, the divinity of Christ and consider their faith to be quite important to them. In their feelings toward their church, however, some showed less enthusiasm. Two in five said they were happy with their churches; a similar proportion, though happy with their church, admitted to a few complaints; the rest revealed increasingly intense degrees of dissatisfaction.

VALUES AND INTERESTS

Among the highest-scoring responses under the general title of "adventure" were "exploring the unknown," "working in an adventurous occupation," "being a prosperous businessman or woman," "being a recognized leader," "discovering a new idea or making an invention," "owning more than one car," "having a good job with lots of free time," and "entering a high-paying profession."

Similarly, a high percentage of Southern Baptist Youth look for meaning in life. Of the random sampling, over half want to arrive at a sound philosophy of life; 50 percent want to help remove social injustice; 42 percent are interested in serving in some church-related vocation; over half want time for reading and reflection; a striking 75 percent (86 percent of assembly Youth) want to be used to help others know Christ; and about two-thirds indicated real interest in meeting interesting people and seeing new places.

Perhaps the most significantly high response appeared in the expressed desire of 86 percent of the random sampling (94 percent of assembly) to accomplish God's will for their lives. Seventy percent of the group want to live lives of unselfish service to man. Eighty-one percent want a college education. Coupled together, these three responses indicate highly-motivated, highly-committed youth.

BELIEFS OF ADULTS AND YOUTH COMPARED

Workers with Youth were asked to take part in the survey so that comparisons could be made with Youth.

Is the question of science as opposed to Christianity a problem? Eighteen percent of adult workers feel that the two oppose each other and another eleven percent responded were uncertain, while one fourth of the Youth in the random sampling feel the same way.

In the area of race relations, 47 percent of the youth and 38 percent of adult workers felt that there is no essential difference between Negroes and whites and that the two races should mingle together socially. Another 12 and 7 percent, respectively, were in doubt. Opposed to such mixing were 41 percent of the Youth and 55 percent of the adults. A significant difference was revealed among the three groups tested with the statement: "The elimination of all racial discrimination is a goal of Christianity." Fifty-seven percent of the Youth in the random sampling, 65 percent of the adult workers, and 97 percent of the assembly Youth said "yes" to this question. The difference in attitude between random and assembly youth is significant.

Other responses: among both adults and youth, the large majority felt that good citizenship requires an interest in government. Other responses from the random sampling of Youth are as follows; 90 percent said that to know Christ is to know God; 90 percent said that even though a Christian sins, he remains a child of God; Christ was tempted just as we are by impure thoughts, resentment and pride: 78 percent; 85 percent said that joining the church is the public confession of one's faith and one's decision to live in Christ; 84 percent, being forgiven by God means also that the Christian is willing to forgive those who have wronged him; 70 percent felt that God calls people to vocations that are not church related; 91 percent felt that after death there is heaven or hell for every person; 71 percent felt that the conversion of a sinner is a greater miracle than the healing of cancer.

Through an evaluation of responses to 80 items, some highly significant factors became apparent. Although 9 percent agreed that "after death there is heaven or hell for every person," 30 percent indicated that "a God of love will not allow people to suffer in hell."

Although traditional concepts of salvation through Christ were accepted by the great majority of Youth, 63 percent feel that "salvation depends upon being sincere in whatever you believe"; 39 percent feel that if one is tolerant, he must hold that other religions are as right before God as Christianity. Thirty-one percent feel that "if I say I believe in God and do right, I will get to heaven." Sixty percent feel that "God is satisfied if a person lives the best life he can." Thirty percent believe that although there are many religions in the world, each one leads to the same God. And 20 percent feel that in matters of religion it really does not matter what one believes.

How about their attitudes toward other denominations?

Fifty-one percent feel that "although there are many denominations—church bodies—the existing differences are insignificant to me as a Christian."

There is a problem among Youth as to how forgiveness is understood. While traditional Baptist doctrine of salvation is embraced by most Youth, these responses indicate that the doctrine has not been appropriated into their life streams: A Christian is forgiven for only those sins for which he specifically asks forgiveness: 32 percent. A person is forgiven only when he feels right in his heart: 44 percent. "As a believer in Christ, I live in complete forgiveness of sin 24 hours daily": 38 percent. There are some sins so bad that God won't forgive them: 15 percent. "I can hope to be saved, but I cannot be certain I am saved": 26 percent. In contrast to these responses, 82 percent agreed that since a Christian's hope is based on what Jesus Christ has done, he can be sure of God's love even if he sins; and another 92 percent said "I believe God forgives my sins."

Southern Baptist Youth indicate a desire for their churches to become involved in more ways with solutions to problems of society. Forty-eight percent said that churches should involve themselves more in social, political, and economic issues. Seventy-five percent said they would like to see their local churches cooperate more with churches of other denominations.

An additional interest in response came to the question "Serving in the armed forces is the responsibility of every American young man who is qualified to do so." Eighty-eight percent agreed with this statement (93 percent of conference Youth said "yes").

ATTITUDES TOWARD YOUTH GROUPS

Youth seem to be generally pleased with their Youth groups. Of the random sampling, 80 percent of the Youth feel that members are full of fun and have good sense of humor; 82 percent feel that everyone is given opportunity to participate; 80

percent indicated that members are friends during the week; and 71 percent feel that adult leaders work faithfully with the members. 59 percent of the Youth report that their ministers "attend our meetings and give helpful guidance." About half feel that a continual effort is made to improve their groups; 52 percent felt that they had interesting social and recreational activities.

Significantly, only 43 percent feel at ease in expressing their Christian experiences to their Youth group. Even more serious is the fact that only 29 percent feel that "it is easy to share and discuss my personal problems when together."

Comparative Profiles of Youth

During the same months, the survey was being conducted among Southern Baptist Youth, the same tools, adapted to the particular denominations, were being used in surveys conducted by the Mennonites and by the Church of God. Dr. Strommen was consultant in these surveys, also, and made comparisons of all the groups surveyed. A fourth denomination—Lutheran—is also included in the comparison, although the survey was conducted in 1963. Some significant differences are apparent.

In areas of concern, Southern Baptist Youth have more difficulty with dating and emotions, concern over a life partner, lack of self-confidence, relationship to teachers, and personal faults than any group surveyed.

In spite of the problems Southern Baptist Youth have with self-assurance, they revealed a greater degree of Youth group spirit and of interest in religious activities than any group tested.

Southern Baptist Youth have a greater problem relating to their teachers than the youth of other denominations tested. About one-third of Southern Baptist Youth feel that "some teachers act as though a teen-ager knows absolutely nothing"; about one-fourth feel that some of their teachers are unfair. Many felt that their teachers were sarcastic and critical of them and disinterested in them. Almost half of Southern Baptist Youth felt that recreation in school that all can enjoy was a very serious problem.

This type of attitude is revealed toward other adults as well as teachers. Southern Baptist Youth, more than any group tested, feel blamed for things they do not do. They feel that some members of their churches are always criticizing. They feel that adults tend to underestimate the abilities of young people. Southern Baptist Youth also revealed their lack of confidence in church adults. Almost one-fourth felt that adults attend church to make an impression. Over half see as a serious problem the fact that "some adults in my community are always saying one thing and doing another."

Southern Baptist Youth also revealed more problems in their relationships with parents than any other group. Over one-third felt that their parents often forget how it feels to be young. Almost half feel they cannot discuss problems with their mothers. About one-third feels nagged much of the time. Over one-fourth feel little closeness with family members. Over one-third sense a much greater need for a feeling of love in their families. Almost half felt that their families should be much happier. About one-fourth feel that their parents frequently try to pry into the Youth's private life. Almost one-fourth, on the other hand, felt that their mothers are not as interested in them as they would like. Almost one-fourth feel that how their parents get along together is a fairly serious problem.

Turning attention to the Youth's relationship with his own age group, more startling information is revealed. Not only do Southern Baptist Youth feel they cannot talk to adults, neither do they feel they can talk with their own peer groups. Almost half feel that classmates at school could be more friendly. Almost as many frequently feel that they are too axious to please others. About one-third feel seriously unable to discuss their faith with their dates. Half of the Youth were greatly concerned about how to keep boys and girls interested in them. About one-third feel that it is hard to be conscious of Christ's presence when on a date.

All areas of relationship are interrelated. It can be assumed that a Youth's attitude toward teachers and church adults and parents will affect his peer relationships. Central to his relationships with others is a person's attitude toward himself.

A significant percentage of Southern Baptist Youth have problems with lack of self-confidence and feelings of insecurity. These are more intense problem areas among Southern Baptist Youth than any group surveyed.

Southern Baptist Youth indicate that they "worry about little things." A proportionately large number, compared with other denominations, are afraid of failure or humiliation. A greater percentage feel that classmates are inconsiderate of their feelings. Almost twice as high a percentage as other groups tested indicated they cannot forgive themselves for things they have done. A larger percentage than other groups indicated concern over their intelligence. A disproportionate percentage indicated frequently feeling that they were not living up to their convictions (which could be a sign of low ego strength and high ideals). An alarming percentage (43 percent) said they were much bothered (very much or quite a bit) with thoughts about dying or being killed. Fifty three percent often wish strongly that they could "get away from it all." Southern Baptist Youth are overly concerned about their studies, getting their feelings hurt, lack of ability, and overconsciousness of personal faults when compared with other groups. They also feel that they "day-dream too much," feel restless, are concerned about personal appearance, "get into moods where they can't cheer up," and feel lonely.

A difficult area to evaluate regards choice of a life partner. Southern Baptist Youth are more concerned than other groups about "what to look for in a life partner"; about whether they will marry someone who will give them happiness; about whether they will find the life partner God wants them to have;

and about finding a life partner who is morally chaste. These reponses can be considered areas of concern through which God may speak to a person. However, some responses indicate uncertainty related to finding the right life partner. A proportionately high percentage of Southern Baptist Youth have difficulty thinking of sex as sacred. They "fall in love too fast." A percentage almost double that of other groups indicated that they cannot stop liking the one with whom they broke up—another indication that adjustment is difficult.

Southern Baptist Youth, more so than other groups, showed concern that "they did not know their Bible as they should," "wish they had a deeper faith in God," and "do not feel as close to God as they should."

What Are Youth Interested In?

Some responses on the questionnaire revealed areas of study which Southern Baptist Youth desire. Boy-girl relationships were of great interest to them. About two-thirds indicated "much interest" in studying the Bible and Christian teachings about relationships between the sexes. Over half wanted counseling or group discussion on sex. When those are added who indicated "some interest" in these subjects, the percentage increases greatly.

About two-thirds showed much interest in finding out what other faiths teach, finding ways to live so that witnessing would be more effective, finding guidance for deciding God's will in life and for developing prayer life and devotions. Two areas of interest topped all the rest: "To learn to know and understand the Bible better" and "To find a closer relationship with God," both of which were requested by 75 percent of Southern Baptist Youth.

Southern Baptist Youth want friendship and encouragement from Christian adults they "can count on." They want to develop greater ability to show love and concern for others (near and far away). They want to develop more meaningful friendships. They want to find meaning and purpose in life, as well as ways to apply their religion to everyday problems.

Summary

In a day of social unrest and widespread restiveness with inflexible forms, the church can demonstrate a positive approach by taking the lead in rethinking traditional approaches to Youth. The study makes it apparent that doors must be opened to greater interaction and exchange between Youth and adults. Each can learn from the other if freedom and acceptance are offered Youth as they are encouraged to air their questions, doubts, struggles, and suggestions. The direction needed is a model of mutuality where the interchange is not sought through more activities (excellent for building institutional loyalties and friendships) but in-depth encounters where "deep-speaks-to-deep" in meaningful ways. It is a truism that one comes to know himself through sharing himself with others. A second accent should build on the loyalty and love the Youth feel toward their congregational fellowship. These Youth who are increasingly concerned about world issues, and will be more involved in community and inter-church activities, will become increasingly critical of lay adults in their congregations who wish to repeat mistakes of the past. Channels need to be encouraged which enable Youth to live out their sense of mission within church structures and have a part in finding new ways of sharing an ageless message. Because change will come through this second accent, a model of mutual tension and conflict must be expected. If Youth and adults are helped to examine new issues in a spirit of love, freedom, and mutual respect, the changes can be interpreted as the work of God's spirit.

---

1. Joe Haynes, then program design and research consultant for the Youth Section of the Sunday School Department, was given responsibility to direct the project. James Lowry of the Research and Statistics Department, was assigned to the project as project analyst.

Dr. Merton Strommen, director of Church Youth Research, was retained as special consultant. Dr. Strommen has pioneered in researching youth.

In 1963 he published *Profiles of Church Youth*, a thorough report of his research on Lutheran church youth. The value of his findings was apparent. Dr. Strommen (a Lutheran minister now devoting full time to youth research) used a questionnaire composed of 400 items. This same questionnaire, because of its validity as a research tool, was adapted and "baptized" with Southern Baptist terminology and viewpoints and used as the primary research tool for this survey.

Dr. Strommen served as consultant at various stages throughout the project, and prepared a report from the results given by computer. This report was thoroughly questioned and evaluated by personnel of the Sunday School Board.

Dr. Strommen insisted throughout the evaluation process that it was one thing to discover and report on characteristics of youth, but quite another thing to draw implications from the survey. The results of the survey present factual information. These facts may be accepted as valid. However, when an evaluator begins to define reasons for the facts, or when he attempts to decide what changes should be made in working with or teaching Southern Baptist Youth, he enters the world of subjectivism. His own viewpoints on life, his previously formed view of youth, his own personality, and numerous other subjective factors enter into his evaluation.

Others who evaluate the research findings should keep in mind these same two matters: that the survey reveals *facts* about youth which must be considered adequately and honestly; and that any evaluation must of necessity be subjective.

For purposes of the survey, churches were divided into four sizes according to [adult] membership: 50 to 199, 200 to 499, 500 to 999, and 1,000 and over. Of the first group, one church out of every 600 was surveyed (a ratio of 1 in 400 was attempted, but due to various factors, all did not participate. Of the second group, 1 church in every 400 was surveyed. Of the third group, 1 church in every 200. Of the fourth group, 1 church in every 100. To give each youth in the Southern Baptist Convention approximately the same chance of being included in the survey the ratio of *youth* surveyed was somewhat different. Effort was made to survey *every* youth of churches in the first two groups; 50 percent of youth in the third group; and 25 percent of the youth in the fourth group. Churches were divided in the survey in accordance with their numbers into four regions—southeast, southwest, west, and north—according to the population density of Southern Baptists. Thus, those regions in which Southern Baptists are strongest were represented. After the churches had been divided into categories of size and region, they were then picked at random. The participating churches in which only 50 percent or 25 percent of youth were surveyed, sent a list of names of all their church youth (less active as well as more active) to the survey directors. The directors then—consistently—circled every second or fourth name on each list. The circled names were the youth designated for the survey. No substitutions were allowed, because the survey was to be of *all* Southern Baptist Youth—not just the faithful.

Personal Learning Activities

Chapter 1

1. What are four concerns of the adolescent?
2. Name two reasons why the youth's struggle for self-identity is difficult in today's world.
3. List three views the adolescent has of himself and briefly explain the significance of each one.

Chapter 2

1. Describe the circumstances which produce acne.
2. True or False: Every youth has an individual pattern of growth unique to him.
3. List several physical changes which take place in sexual maturation.
4. What are four excessives which often result from rapid physical growth?

Chapter 3

1. What is the significance of bad manners and emotional unpredictability in the youth?
2. List five typical fears of adolescent girls.
3. Why should a youth feel loved by his parents?

Chapter 4

1. Name three foundations for brainpower.
2. List nine specific areas of mental development.
3. What is a major change accuring in education today?

Chapter 5

1. What are some conflicts in parent-youth relationships during youth's emancipation period?
2. What difficulties are presented between parents and youth by the sexual barrier?
3. Name four special family problems faced by some youth.

Chapter 6

1. What are four factors which influence a youth's choice of friends?
2. Name six values of the clique.
3. Name three negatives of the clique.
4. What significance is the "crush" to the younger youth?

Chapter 7

1. What is the youth subculture?
2. Name several ways business attempts to capitalize on the youth subculture.
3. What are some causes for the communication gap being wider now than in former generations?

Chapter 8

1. What is studenthood?
2. Name three directions from which pressure comes for good grades.
3. How can churches guide youth to make good vocational choices?

Chapter 9

1. List eight causes for youth to drop out of school.
2. What is a vitally important factor in the church's ministry to drop-outs?

Chapter 10

1. List four characteristics of youth's music.
2. Name five areas of social concern of particular importance to youth.

Chapter 11
1. What are four concepts youth might have of religion?
2. How does a youth's feelings toward his parents influence his religious development?
3. According to Strang, what is the most pressing intellectual problem facing youth today?
4. List seven guidelines for leading youth in religious development.

Chapter 12
1. List three "common ventures of life" about which youth must make decisions.
2. What are four guidelines for assisting youth in educational and vocational choices?

The New Church Study Course

THE New Church Study Course effective in January 1970 is based on more than three years of study and design. It offers several improvements in the Church Study Course, which began in October 1959. At that time three courses previously promoted by the Sunday School Board were merged: the Sunday School Training Course, the Graded Training Union Study Course, and the Church Music Training Course. Principles and methods books of the Woman's Missionary Union and the Brotherhood Commission were added in October 1961 and January 1967 respectively.

The New Church Study Course offers increased flexibility in meeting the needs of Southern Baptists. It provides courses of varying length and difficulty, varied formats and types of course materials, additional types of credit, and improved organization of courses.

The New Church Study Course consists of two types of courses: the Christian Development Courses for all church members, and the Christian Leadership Courses for church leaders. Courses are organized into subject areas.

The purpose of the Christian Development Courses is to provide courses of study which will help church members grow toward maturity in Christian living and competence in Christian service. These courses offer more comprehensive, advanced, and varied learning experiences in subject areas of a church's educational program than can be provided through curriculum periodicals. Tests and exercises, credits, and diplomas of achievement which help church members measure their progress in developing needed knowledge, understanding, and skills are included in some courses. Units of instruction are provided for Preschoolers and Children. These are designed to reinforce foundational learnings. Materials which churches may use in recognizing the participation of Preschoolers and Children in these units are available from Baptist Book Stores.

The Christian Leadership Courses provide a comprehensive series of courses organized into subject areas dealing with knowledge, understandings, and skills needed for effective church leadership. Tests and exercises, credits and diplomas to help leaders measure their growth in leadership ability are included in some courses. The Christian Leadership Courses are the primary source for leadership training materials prepared by the agencies cooperating in the New Church Study Course.

Courses of both types are designed to be effective for individual and class study. Learning aids, study guides, and teaching guides are available for some courses. Credits are granted to Youth and Adults for reading, individual study, and class study.

The New Church Study Course is promoted by the Sunday School Board, 127 Ninth Avenue, North, Nashville, Tennessee 37203, through the departments in the Education Division; by the Woman's Missionary Union, 600 North Twentieth Street, Birmingham, Alabama 35203; by the Brotherhood Commission, 1548 Poplar Avenue, Memphis, Tennessee 38104; and by the respective departments in the state conventions affiliated with the Southern Baptist Convention.

A record of all credits and diplomas earned should be maintained in each church.

Detailed information about the course and the system of credits, diplomas, and record keeping is available from the agencies listed above.

Forms for keeping records may be ordered from any Baptist Book Store.

Requirements for Credit

This book is the text for course 5161-03 of subject area 61 of the Christian Development Courses, New Church Study Course. If credit is desired for this course through class study, individual study, or reading, the following requirements must be met:

I. CLASS WORK

1. This course is designed for ten (10) hours of class study and carries four credits for such usage. If the course is studied in a class setting of less than ten (10) hours, the following criteria apply:
   (1) Seven and one half (7½) class hours—three (3) credits
   (2) Five (5) class hours—two (2) credits
   (3) Two and one half class hours—one (1) credit
   The teacher will indicate the length of the class and the number of credits to be granted on the "Request for Course Credit" (Form 151).

2. A class member who attends all class sessions and completes the reading of the book as directed by the teacher will not be required to do any written work for credit.

3. A class member who is absent from one or more sessions must complete the required exercises or question in the "Personal Learning Activities" section on all chapters he misses. In such a case, he must turn in his paper by the date the teacher sets (usually within ten days following the last class). Also, he must certify that he has read the book.

4. The teacher should request an award for himself. A person who teaches a course for Youth or Adults (in any subject area) will be granted the same number of credits as class members. The teacher of an approved unit of study for Preschoolers and Children will be

granted two credits for course 2299 in subject area 22 of the Christian Leadership Series. Request award by using Form 151.

5. The director of Church Training or the teacher of the course should complete the "Request for Course Credit" (Form 151) and forward it after completion of the class to the Church Study Course Awards Office, 127 Ninth Avenue, North, Nashville, Tennessee 37203.

II. INDIVIDUAL STUDY

1. A person who wishes to complete this course without attending class session may receive full credit by certifying that he has read the book and by completing all exercises or questions in the "Personal Learning Activities" section.

2. Students may find profit in studying the text together, but individual papers are required. Carbon copies or duplicates of the answers cannot be accepted.

3. The work required for individual study credit should be turned in for checking to the director of Church Training or the person designated by the church to administer the Christian Leadership Courses. The form entitled "Request for Course Credit" (Form 151) must be used in requesting these awards. It is to be forwarded by the director of Church Training or the person designated by the church to the Church Study Course Awards Office, 127 Ninth Avenue, North, Nashville, Tennessee 37203.

III. READING CREDIT

1. A person may receive one credit toward the diploma on which he is working by reading this book.

2. Upon completion of the reading, he must complete the "Request for Course Credit" (Form 151). He should give the completed form to the director of Church Training or to the person designated by his church to be responsible for administering the Christian Leadership Courses.

3. The director of Church Training or the person designated by the church will see that the request is completed, signed, and forwarded to the Church Study Course Awards Office, 127 Ninth Avenue, North, Nashville, Tennessee 37203.

IV. AWARDS AND RECORDS

Two copies of the course credit award form will be sent by the Study Course Awards Office to the church. One copy should be filed in the church training record and the other given to the individual.

Bibliography

Adams, James F. *Understanding Adolescence*. Boston: Allyn and Bacon, Inc., 1968.

Browning, Robert L. *Communicating With Junior Highs*. Nashville: Graded Press, 1968.

Duvall, Evelyn M. *Sex Ways—In Fact and Faith*. New York: Association Press, 1961.

Duvall, Eveyln M. *Today's Teen-Agers*. New York: Association Press, 1966.

Erikson, Eric H. *Identity, Youth and Crisis*. New York: W. W. Norton, 1968.

Ferguson, Rowena. *The Church's Ministry with Senior Highs*. Nashville: The Graded Press, 1963.

Friedenberg, Edgar Z. *Coming of Age in America*. New York: Random House, 1965.

Goldman, Ronald. *Readiness for Religion*. New York: Seabury Press, 1965.

Gordon, Ira J. *Human Development: From Birth Through Adolescence*. New York: Harper and Brothers, Publisher, 1962.

Smith, Ernest A. *American Youth Culture*. Glencoe, Illinois: Glencoe Free Press, 1962.

Stewart, Charles William. *Adolescent Religion*. Nashville: Abingdon Press, 1967.

Strang, Ruth. *The Adolescent Views Himself*. New York: McGraw-Hill Book Company, Inc., 1957.

Strommen, Merton. *Profiles of Church Youth*. St. Louis: Concordia Publishing House, 1963.

Usdin, Gene L. M.D., editor. *Adolescence: Care and Counseling*. Philadelphia: J. B. Lippincott Company, 1967.